# WRITING SHORT STORIES AND ARTICLES

## How To Books on Successful Writing

Copyright & Law for Writers
Creating a Twist in the Tale
Creative Writing
How to be a Freelance Journalist
How to Publish a Book
How to Publish a Newsletter
How to Start Word Processing
How to Write a Press Release
How to Write & Sell Computer
  Software
How to Write for Television
Improving Your Written English
Making Money from Writing
Mastering Business English
Researching for Writers
Starting to Write
Writing & Publishing Poetry

Writing & Selling a Novel
Writing a Nonfiction Book
Writing a Pantomime
Writing a Report
Writing a Textbook
Writing an Assignment
Writing an Essay
Writing Business Letters
Writing Erotic Fiction
Writing for Publication
Writing Reviews
Writing Romantic Fiction
Writing Science Fiction, Fantasy
  & Horror
Writing Short Stories & Articles
Writing Your Dissertation

*Other titles in preparation*

The How To series now contains more than 200 titles in the following categories:

Business & Management
Computer Basics
General Reference
Jobs & Careers
Living & Working Abroad

Personal Finance
Self-Development
Small Business
Student Handbooks
Successful Writing

Please send for a free copy of the latest catalogue for full details (see back cover for address).

## SUCCESSFUL WRITING

# WRITING SHORT STORIES AND ARTICLES

## How to write successfully for magazines and newspapers

### Adèle Ramet

**How To Books**

Cartoons by Simon Ramet

**British Library Cataloguing in Publication Data**

A catalogue record for this book is available from the British Library.

© Copyright 1998 by Adèle Ramet.

First published in 1998 by How To Books Ltd, 3 Newtec Place,
Magdalen Road, Oxford, OX4 1RE, United Kingdom.
Tel: (01865) 793806. Fax: (01865) 248780.

*Note:* The material contained in this book is set out in good faith for
general guidance and no liability can be accepted for loss or expense
incurred as a result of relying in particular circumstances on statements
made in this book. The law and regulations may be complex and liable to
change, and readers should check the current position with the relevant
authorities before making personal arrangements.

Produced for How To Books by Deer Park Productions.
Typeset by Concept Communications (Design & Print) Ltd, Crayford, Kent.
Printed and bound by Cromwell Press, Trowbridge, Wiltshire.

# Contents

## Contents 7

# List of Illustrations

# Preface

## Article or short story?

Newspapers and magazines are two of the most attainable markets for article and short story writers keen to see their work in print.

Many a struggling writer's first taste of success may well have been the letters page of their local newspaper or favourite magazine. Moved to put pen to paper by a local injustice, an amusing incident or just because they enjoy writing letters, the pleasure of being published is invariably addictive.

Once hooked on publication, the true writer will be unable to stop and the letters will begin their inevitable metamorphosis into an article or story. It is at this stage that we need to pause and consider the options open to the freelance contributor.

Bearing in mind that the majority of topical hard news stories are provided by professional journalists and staff writers, this still leaves plenty of scope for the freelance in the form of feature articles and short stories. It is, therefore, extremely useful to develop the ability to write both fact and fiction.

For those writers familiar with journalistic references to news *stories*, the distinction between an article and a story may be unclear. Is it fact or fiction? Indeed, when is a story not a story? At first sight, some of the definitions for the word 'story' given in *Chambers Dictionary* simply add to the confusion:

- a fictitious narrative
- a tale
- an anecdote
- a news article.

However, as every successful freelance knows, the answer to the riddle, 'When is a story not a story?' is probably 'When it's an article'. Whilst the format may differ, the approach by the writer is surprisingly similar.

This book is designed to give writers an insight into both the

9

similarities in and the differences between producing fictional short stories and non-fiction articles for the magazine and newspaper markets. The key to both formats is:

● brevity
● clarity
● reader identification.

One discipline relies heavily on the ability to place factual information in a logical order in a manner that is easily absorbed by the reader. The other requires the writer to have a sound grasp of fiction-writing techniques. As you work your way through this book, however, you will discover that these elements are to be found in varying proportions in both genres.

This book takes you step by step through the techniques of writing both articles and short stories. It shows you how to write to length and style, how to adapt your work for different markets and how the inclusion of fiction techniques can enhance and improve factual articles. Research and the importance of factual accuracy in fiction will be explained and guidance is given on how to present and market your finished manuscripts.

Master the requirements of both genres and you will double your chances of writing successfully for newspapers and magazines.

# Acknowledgements

I would like to thank freelance writers Jill Eckersley, Kate Nivison and Gillian Thornton for their supportive and encouraging words of advice.

My thanks also to Groundwork Bridgend, Linda Sutton and the following editors for their patience and generous co-operation in the writing of this book:

Gaynor Davies of *Woman's Weekly*
Neil Fowler of *The Western Mail*
John Lloyd of *Camping Magazine*
Linda O'Byrne and Sue Preston of *Bella*
Jane O'Neill of *Woman's Journal*
A. Noguera of *FHM*
Dee Nolan of *You*
Jane Weatherall of *Yours*
Adrienne Wild of *Garden Answers*

A very special thank you is due to my family for all their practical support in the writing of this book and for always being there for me when I need them.

*Adèle Ramet*

# 1

# Mixing Fact and Fiction

The motivation to write for publication differs widely from one writer to another. Many start at school, writing essays and stories in their English lessons. Consistently high marks from a teacher they respect in a subject they enjoy may well plant the seed of hope that one day, in the far distant future, they may try their hand at writing a novel.

For others, it is the school magazine that shapes their ambition. A series of articles, possibly leading to them taking over the editor's chair and before you know it, a future non-fiction feature writer is born.

## Picking up the threads

Whilst these early enthusiasms can lead to a career as a professional journalist, the vast majority of us simply place these ambitions in the same unattainable category as rock star or racing driver and go about our more mundane daily lives.

However, for many of us there comes a time, prompted perhaps by redundancy, children leaving home or simply the belief that we can do better than the author of the article or short story we've just read, when our thoughts return to those early writing successes of our schooldays.

Our choice of fact or fiction is invariably influenced by our past interests and eager to pick up the threads where we left off, we feel we have to return to either one or the other. However, just because you were good at articles in the past, doesn't mean you can't write short stories now, and vice versa.

## Understanding the differences

Before we begin to explore the many similarities, it is useful to establish exactly what differences there are between the two genres. The chart in Figure 1 highlights the main points which separate factual articles from fictional short stories.

| Articles | Stories |
|---|---|
| Fact, i.e. the truth | Fiction, i.e. a lie |
| Primarily informative | Primarily entertaining |
| Author can provide own illustrations | Illustrations always provided by magazine |
| Quotations from other published articles add credibility | Quotations from published authors can spoil the fictional flow |
| The ending can be either downbeat or uplifting depending upon the theme and purpose of the article | Most magazine short stories require an upbeat ending |

Fig. 1. The differences between factual articles and fictional stories.

## ESTABLISHING COMMON GROUND

Perhaps the best way to distinguish between the two genres is to remember that fiction writers tell lies whilst article writers tell the truth. Well, most of the time anyway.

Having established the main differences, we now need to look at the common ground. This comes from the techniques the writer needs to employ in order to communicate effectively with the reader.

Short stories and articles both require:

● a beginning, a middle and an ending which ties up satisfactorily with the beginning

● a strong, attention-grabbing opening which gives an indication of what is to follow

● accurate factual information

● clear imagery

● reader identification

● content which reflects the style of the newspaper or magazine for which it is intended.

Both genres must also:

● be written to a pre-determined length

● have an original slant

- hold the reader's attention from beginning to end
- deliver what was promised in the opening line.

One extra ingredient which is optional for the article but is usually considered essential for a short story is:

- a proportion of dialogue.

All these points will be explained as you work through the book, but as you can already see, there are many factors which are common to both genres.

## EXPLOITING THE SIMILARITIES

Having gained an insight into the techniques required to write fact and fiction, we can exploit the similarities to enable us to write productively for newspapers and magazines.

### Beginning with an idea

Imagine the scene. In the hope of selling an article to your local newspaper, you are attending a school fête. A wide variety of animals have been entered for the annual pet show but your attention is drawn to the dogs' obedience competition where, you are told, this year's winner is an ill-treated animal, rescued by the RSPCA.

In addition to a general report on the fête, you now have the opportunity to write a whole range of articles for a selection of outlets, from specialist magazines for dog-owners to mass market publications. There is scope for:

- a feature about the dog and its owner

- a feature about pet shows in general

- a report on the work of the RSPCA

- an in-depth investigation into cruelty to animals

- a step-by-step guide to dog training

- a report highlighting the special problems involved in taking on a rescue pet.

At this stage, you are still only looking at topics associated with dogs but there will have been a range of pets at the show, including some exotic animals which could give rise to all sorts of article ideas.

## Finding a story

The possibilities for articles are extensive but so, too, are the possibilities for fiction.

Pets have a knack of bringing people together and offer any number of situations for romantic fiction. Two lonely people walking their dogs in the park, a kind stranger offering to help rescue a cat from a tree or someone returning a lost pet to its rightful owner.

Animals also provide the opportunity for conflict between their owners and where there is conflict, there is potential not only for romance but also for a twist in the tale.

For example, keen gardeners can be highly intolerant of a neighbour's wandering cat. Where a potentially prize-winning plant is under severe threat from the unwanted attentions of a pedigree pussycat, more than a little fur will fly in the days leading up to the local fête.

## PLAYING AROUND WITH THE FACTS

Earlier in this chapter, I stated that fiction writers tell lies, whilst article writers tell the truth. The truth is, that this statement was a lie.

## Telling lies

Whilst a good article is based firmly in fact, there is nothing wrong with employing one or two fiction-writing tricks of the trade in order to liven up a piece of non-fiction.

You may, for example, be writing a personal experience article about the problems you encountered on your first ever caravan holiday. As the article begins to take shape, you are reminded of an amusing incident which took place on a much later trip.

By this time, you had owned a caravan for several years and were experienced enough to know better but with a little tweaking here and there, the anecdote offers some handy hints on caravan towing and serves to round off the article perfectly.

OK, so maybe you have drastically altered the sequence of events in order to embellish the feature, but politics is not the only profession where being economical with the truth can be highly effective in achieving the desired result.

## READING ABOUT PEOPLE

Whether fact or fiction, people read about people. Factual articles which include case histories, informal chats, quotes and photographs are far more interesting than those which simply list a lot of statistical information.

## Expanding the 'I' element

As article writers, we are advised to write about what we know and in order to establish credibility, we need to include details of our own personal experience. However, one of the biggest pitfalls for the novice writer is the 'I' element, as demonstrated in Example A below:

*Example A*

My first caravan holiday was a total disaster. The first thing I did wrong was to forget to make everything secure for travelling. Then I left the milk behind and I hadn't gone more than a few miles along the motorway before I was pulled over by the police.

By now, any experienced caravanner will have lost patience with the writer and inexperienced readers will have gained no concrete information. This is one person's own story and is of no interest to anyone else.

The first thing the writer needs to do is to replace the word 'I' with the word 'you'. This brings in the element which is essential for both fact and fiction, that of reader identification. In other words, the reader must be able to relate to the people and situations featured in your articles and short stories. The rewritten Example B offers this element to the reader:

*Example B*

If you're planning to tour with a caravan for the first time, you're in for a rare treat. No other holiday combines the same kind of freedom with the luxury a well-equipped caravan provides. That isn't to say that there aren't one or two pitfalls, but by following a few simple rules they can be easily avoided.

In the next chapter, we'll be looking at different types of articles and formats you can use, but the above sample is an illustration of the opening to a straightforward factual information piece.

## CHANGING WITH THE SEASONS

One of the biggest headaches facing an editor is finding suitable features and stories which reflect the changing seasons and significant days throughout the annual calendar.

### Keeping one step ahead

We will be looking at **topicality** later in the book, but for now, bear in mind that the writer whom an editor can call upon to fill a seasonal slot is always in demand. Editors are invariably looking for articles and stories which not only reflect seasonal changes in the weather but also the following events on the annual calendar:

● Christmas

● St Valentine's Day

● Easter

● All Fool's Day

● Mothering Sunday

● Father's Day

● Halloween.

They will also require features commemorating anniversaries of historical events and influential figures, holiday ideas for 'Summer Specials' and educational items for 'Back to School' editions. There will be more information on planning ahead for these issues in Chapter 10.

## TAKING A FLEXIBLE APPROACH

For the short story writer, the magazine market is quite specific. Ages and lifestyles of characters will be heavily influenced by the readership of the magazines at which you are aiming and because magazine styles are very distinctive, the market for any one particular storyline may be quite limited.

As the fiction market is so restrictive, rather than waste good research material by confining it to one or perhaps two short stories, it pays to put any facts you have discovered to good use in the form of a number of different articles.

### Getting the most out of the material

Never allow anything to go to waste. Your cupboards and drawers will quickly become stuffed with newspaper cuttings, press releases, information leaflets and any other useful material you can lay your hands on, but it will be worth it in the end.

It certainly pays to be flexible. Set out all the facts you have available, the seasonal implications, the people involved, then consider the uses to which you can put all the information. Fact, fiction or a mixture of both, anything's worth a try.

## CASE STUDIES

### George tells his story

George has led a full and active life and since his retirement, has taken up a number of hobbies. His anecdotes about his work and the people he meets in pursuit of his interests are fun to listen to but are far too personal to interest anyone who does not know him. He uses the word 'I' constantly and until he stands back from the incidents he relates and puts them in a broader context, he will fail in his bid to achieve publication.

### John shares his expertise

John is an office worker in his late thirties. Like George, he has several hobbies about which he is both enthusiastic and knowledgeable. His articles and short stories are always written with a specific readership in mind and are designed both to inform and to entertain. His subject expertise brings an authority to his work which adds an important dimension to everything that he writes.

## CHECKLIST

1. Are you sure you know the difference between an article and a short story?

2. Do you have sufficient factual information for an article?

3. Can you turn some of your facts into a short story?

4. Does the word 'you' feature significantly in your article?

5. Will a reader relate to the people and situations you are writing about?

## ASSIGNMENT

Think of a single theme based on your own interest and expertise and write down as many different article ideas as you can. When you've finished, go back and see how many of those ideas could be adapted into fictional short stories.

# 2
# Constructing an Article

## HOOKING THE READER

When you sit down to write an article, there are two main points to keep in mind:

1. the topic you are writing about

2. the person who will read it.

### Selecting the right topics

There is no doubt that you will get better results if you write about what you know rather than if you attempt to write authoritatively on a subject with which you are unfamiliar.

### Writing for the reader

The key to writing effective articles is not to write for yourself but to inform and entertain the reader.

Let's say that your hobby is decorating eggs and you want to write an article about it. Don't be tempted to set up the background in a lengthy introduction about yourself or your reader will have completely lost interest by the time the topic is revealed.

### Grabbing the reader's attention

If you are to grab and hold a reader's attention, it is essential to tell them what the article is about in the very first line. A good opening should:

● be short and to the point

● tell you the topic in the first line

● give you a hint of what is to come.

To illustrate the point, which of the following two openings would make you want to read on?

*Opening A*
I began my hobby many years ago when my parents took me on holiday to a tiny village in the country. However, it was many years later before I was able to take it up, long after my family had grown up and left home and I was able to devote more time to my own hobbies and interests. It took me ages to gather together the materials I needed, find a place to store them and clear a space in the house for me to work and then a close relative became ill and I had to help look after them, so that put paid to any plans of my own.

*Opening B*
With a final brush stroke, Sheila's latest work is complete and she adds a highly decorative goose egg to her large collection of handpainted eggs.
Sheila began decorating eggs over thirty years ago. She uses mainly chicken and goose eggs but before she starts a new design, the first step is to blow and clean her 'canvas'.

In Opening A, the first line fails to reveal the subject of the article and you are none the wiser by the end of the paragraph. No editor would bother reading beyond this point, but should the piece somehow find its way into print, few readers would be persuaded to struggle on.

Opening B, on the other hand, gives you the topic in the first sentence. It introduces a person with whom the reader can identify and you have an indication that the article will be a step-by-step introduction to egg decoration.

An article of this type would be most suitable for either a local interest or a craft/hobby publication. In this case, your reader will be a person who enjoys arts and crafts and will expect concrete information about the topic, not a rambling piece detailing the life and times of someone they have never met.

## Learning something new

Providing you choose subjects you find interesting, there is no reason why you shouldn't research and write about topics you know little about. Just bear in mind that an article you find boring to write will be even more boring for a stranger to read. Because people read about people, you can enliven the piece with the inclusion of a little background information about the person practising the craft and some dialogue with them.

## DRAFTING AN OUTLINE

Having decided upon a topic, it is worth taking the time to sort out exactly what points you intend to cover. Writing an outline along the lines of the one shown in Figure 2 will give you a framework for the piece and keep your mind focused on the task in hand. As we shall see later in this chapter, it is all too easy to wander away from the main theme and an outline should prevent this.

## KEEPING TO THE POINT

An outline should be treated as a flexible framework on which to base your article. Once devised, the next stage is to consider the content in more detail and this is where your mind has a habit of wandering off the point.

| BEGINNING | Introduction to the craft, history, popularity and to Sheila, the artist. |
|-----------|---------------------------------------------------------------------------|
| MIDDLE | Sheila's background. |
| | Egg decorating step by step. |
| | Explain how reader can get started and lead in to closing paragraphs. |
| END | Materials, stockists, costs, courses, reference books, useful addresses and contact numbers, etc. |
| | Tie up with opening. |

Fig. 2. Sample outline for article on egg decorating.

### Condensing the content

Having opened the egg decorating article quite economically, we have set the tone for a straight, no-frills, information piece.

Using the outline in Figure 2 as a guide, the middle paragraphs should not only contain a factual guide to egg painting but also some personal information about Sheila and some dialogue with her. This should be as brief as possible but with sufficient detail to satisfy the reader's natural curiosity and establish Sheila's credibility as a skilled practitioner of her craft. Something along the following lines would be suitable:

Sheila has been decorating eggs for over thirty years and still has the first one she ever attempted at the age of 14. On leaving college, she worked as an art teacher for several years before staying at home to bring up her family.

'During this period,' she explained, 'I had time to develop my egg decorating skills and was eventually approached to run classes at my local community centre.'

In addition to teaching, Sheila now offers her highly decorative eggs for sale in a number of specialist outlets throughout the country . . .

Link the middle and the closing paragraphs with something like, 'Sheila advises anyone interested in taking up the hobby to . . .', and go on to list the steps the reader should take.

Referring once more to the outline, you can see that the following practical reference information should be given in the concluding paragraphs:

● materials and costs

● stockists (including mail order details)

● addresses (including telephone numbers) of courses, and costs if available

● useful books including details of publishers and prices.

## Rounding off the piece

Finally, the article should be brought to a close by rounding it off with a reference to the opening. For example, the following paragraph closes the piece by mirroring the opening references to Sheila and the topic itself:

For Sheila, knowing that people are prepared to buy her work is an added bonus. The true satisfaction is seeing a humble hen's egg transformed into a decorative work of art.

## LAYING IT OUT LOGICALLY

With the sort of subject matter featured in the egg decorating example, putting the information in a logical order is relatively simple.

## Piecing it all together

Having settled on a topic and a suitable readership, the format for the article was quite straightforward, but this isn't always the case.

The subject you have in mind might be 'Life in Eighteenth-Century England' or 'Mythical Beasts Throughout The Ages'. These are such broad headings that without a clear outline, set out in a logical order, you could end up in a terrible muddle.

In order to ensure that you are working logically, draft out a sensible framework in the form of a step-by-step outline. Discard anything that leads you away from the main theme, but retain the details for future use. One good, strong article can become the first of a series if you use the material wisely.

Before you begin, establish exactly which points you wish to cover, then place them in the sequence you feel is the most logical. For example, you may consider that chronological order would be the most sensible for an article on mythical beasts, so the sequence might be along the following lines:

1.  the first recorded mythical creatures

2.  the physical forms they have taken down the ages

3.  examples of the forms in which various images have been represented, i.e. paintings, statues, etc.

4.  examples of beasts which have a special religious significance

5.  some twentieth-century equivalents.

## Varying the format

The above sequence takes the reader logically through the subject and ties the ending up with the beginning by making a 'then and now' comparison.

You may feel, however, that a different order would be more appropriate. Perhaps you would prefer to concentrate on the artistic representations or religious significance. Another angle might be to compare each mythical beast with a possible real-life counterpart.

Whichever aspect you select, providing you stick firmly to the theme of the article and work towards bringing the ending back round to the beginning, you will achieve a satisfactory result.

## WORKING TO A SET LENGTH

Writing for the mainstream press always involves writing to a set length. The publications all have:

● a set number of pages

● a predetermined amount of column inches

● a specific policy regarding illustrations

● a set format which is familiar to the readership.

Each article has to be designed to fit a specific slot within the magazine's format and the required information must be delivered within a predetermined number of words.

## Specialising to start you off

The above rules always apply to mainstream titles, but there are a great many specialist and amateur publications which welcome articles from good freelance writers. Although many are restricted by cost to a limited number of pages, they can be far more flexible in the amount of space they are prepared to devote to a new contributor. The down side to this is that payment usually ranges from very low to non-existent, but for many new writers, simply seeing their 5,000-word article in print is sufficient reward.

By contrast, experienced freelances will invariably expect the full National Union of Journalists (NUJ) rate per word for their contributions and they probably have a fair point. It is, however, worth bearing in mind that small circulation publications can sometimes prove extremely useful to the novice writer in providing both experience and a portfolio of published work.

## Making it fit the space provided

Assuming that your article is for a mainstream publication, you must know the required number of words. If the allotted space requires, say, 1,000 words, your article should ideally be as close to that limit as possible, somewhere between 900 and 1,100 words. Substantially less or more than the given figure and the editor will have their work cut out shaping the piece to fit its slot. At best, your article will be cut to ribbons and at worst, the editor will never use you again.

## Turning the words around

When cutting a piece that is too long, it's a lovely but misguided thought that all you have to do is simply remove a few words here and there. Whilst you can sometimes get away with cutting out a few chunks of superfluous information, more often than not your best course of action is to find a better way to use the few words you have. This involves careful use of vocabulary, turning words and phrases around so that the piece reads more clearly, and never using two words when one will do.

See if you can cut the following piece without losing any of the information it contains, rephrasing and altering the vocabulary where necessary:

> I don't know about you but I love cats and I can't tell you how exciting I find the prospect of obtaining a new kitten. There are lots of things you have to remember to do before the kitten arrives. In the first place,

you have to buy three dishes, one for water, which should have a solid base so that you can't upset it easily, one for food and one for milk. Oh, by the way, I should have mentioned that the water must be cool and of course, it has to be clean and you should throw away stale water and refill the bowl with fresh water every day. (111 words)

Shortened rewrite at end of book page 138.

## Assessing the length

Even in today's high-tech age of electronic word counts on PCs and word processors, many experienced writers still prefer to assess the length of a piece by the number of double-spaced typed A4 pages it covers. A very rough guide is that a double-line spaced A4 typewritten or word-processed page, with 3cm right- and left-hand margins, should amount to between 250 and 290 words.

Once you have established the word length per page, experience will eventually tell you when and where you need to start wrapping up the article you are writing.

## Less is more

It is always far better to have too much material than too little. Write the piece to its natural length, then bring it down to the correct wordage by cutting out any superfluous words and detail.

If the article comes up too short, never be tempted to 'pad' it out with flowery description or irrelevant information. Re-read it to see if you've left anything out. If you can't find anything to fill the gap, then it may be that you don't have enough knowledge of your chosen topic to form the basis of an article. If this is the case, then put the idea aside until you have carried out more research and choose something else to write about.

## CASE STUDIES

### Sue tells you about herself

Sue is keen to write about her collection of antique china, but after typing out fifteen pages she can't think of anything more to write. Having given a rambling account of how she got started when a friend took her to a country house auction, she has run out of steam before giving any solid information about the antiques she collects.

### Paul sets out the facts

Paul, a mechanic in his early fifties, is a vintage car enthusiast and has been involved in several restoration projects. He writes an article giving a step-by-step account of one such restoration, beginning with a brief history of the vehicle and ending with its modern equivalent. The finished article is accepted for publication in the specialist car magazine he has subscribed to for several years.

## CHECKLIST

1. Does your article have an attention-grabbing opening?
2. Does your opening give a clear indication of what is to come?
3. Is the middle informative and interesting?
4. Does the ending tie up with the beginning?
5. Do you keep to the point from beginning to end?

## ASSIGNMENT

Select a magazine which specialises in your subject area and see if you can write an article which will fit into its format and house style. Establish the required length by physically counting the words in articles published in the magazine.

Does your article have an attention-grabbing opening?

# 3
# Getting Articles into Print

## WRITING FEATURES FOR MAGAZINES

Mainstream or specialist, the market for features is wide and varied.
A feature article could be any one of the following:

- a 'think' piece commenting on an aspect of life relevant to your readership
- a 'reader's true story'
- a step-by-step 'how to' article
- a local or specialist interest piece ⟩
- an information piece, such as a travel article.

### Freelancing as a professional

Taking the above examples one by one, 'think' pieces commenting on the idiosyncrasies of life in general are rarely written by unknown contributors.

This type of editorial tends to be staff-written by a senior editor, professional journalist or well-known personality. However, a thought-provoking article on a topically controversial subject could find its way into print. Factual accuracy combined with real-life examples could be developed into a discussion feature especially if it relates directly to the lives of the readers.

Features editor Sue Preston of *Bella* magazine commissions discussion articles of this type for their **Reports, Talking Points** and **Hot Topics** features. Whilst she welcomes subject ideas, these should be accompanied by an outline of how the feature would develop. Working knowledge of the magazine's style and format is essential if your suggestion is to be seriously considered.

### Sinning, confessing and repenting

There are plenty of openings in the women's magazine market for readers' true tales, life-changing experiences, amazing escapes, daring feats of bravery and, of course, the classic 'sin, confess and repent' stories which are an integral feature of many weekly magazines. These personal interest stories are gleaned from a variety of sources:

● news agencies

● local newspapers

● help organisations

● sent in by readers.

Whilst some are pure sensationalism, most are designed to offer messages of hope to readers experiencing similar traumas in their lives.

Although many are staff-written, there are always openings for freelances who can write readers' true tales to a professional standard, but be aware when submitting your own personal confession story that, should it be accepted for publication, it will almost certainly be rewritten by a professional writer before it appears in print.

## Sharing information

General information and 'how to' articles are perhaps marginally easier to place. The market for these is very wide and there is always room for the expert who can write clearly and informatively about his or her specialist subject.

## Utilising local knowledge, arts and crafts

Regional publications are always on the lookout for specialist pieces with a local flavour, particularly if they highlight an item of unusual historical significance or are designed to publicise a forthcoming event.

Arts and craft articles will find a home not only in subject specific magazines, but also, where a thriving small business is concerned, in local newspapers and county magazines. Good subjects for such features would be designers and manufacturers of:

● hand-made pots

● quality furniture

● stained-glass windows

● novelty goods.

## Finding a market

There are literally thousands of magazines currently on sale in the UK, only a small fraction of which are on display in newsagents and supermarkets. A large proportion of specialist publications have to be ordered or are obtained by subscription.

In addition to the well-known mainstream titles, listed below are just a few of the categories for specialist publications currently on the market.

● antiques

● brides and weddings

● business matters

● cars

● computers

● country matters

● environmental issues

● hair care and styling

● high fashion

● home improvement

● pets

● sport

● stamp collecting

● steam engines.

## Playing the field

There simply isn't room in this book to list every single subject area, but in addition to the markets mentioned above, there is a less well-documented one in the form of magazines and newsletters produced by local schools, clubs, organisations and religious groups. Whilst they rarely offer any financial reward, these publications can provide a superb training ground for the new writer and lead them on to more lucrative opportunities.

## Travelling and trekking

Travel articles range from short snippets about family day trips to thousands of words recounting the perils of backpacking through treacherous terrain in some far flung corner of the world.

When it comes to passing on your personal holiday experiences, whilst the backpacking one might be considered, consign the story of last year's package tour to Benidorm to the bin now, while you're ahead.

If you intend to write travel articles for publication, you will need at least some, if not all, of the following:

● knowledge of and contacts in the travel industry

● wide travelling experience

● current factual information about the holidays and locations you feature

● access to up-to-the-minute market information

● the ability to tailor the content and format to individual editorial requirements.

Although it is a specialist professional area, if you can fulfil the above criteria, then it is well worth giving travel-writing a try. As with any other form of feature writing, there is always room for a fresh, new voice.

## KNOWING YOUR SUBJECT

The advice to 'write about what you know' may appear to be rather obvious but in the world of the feature article, this may not be as straightforward as it seems.

### Keeping up with the times

In order to write informative, factual articles, it is essential that you keep up with innovations in your chosen field. For example, your feature may be a relatively abstract one telling the story of how you coped with bereavement — a very personal experience which you hope will help your readers come to terms with a similar loss in their own lives. In addition to describing your own emotions, the article should also contain some or all of the following:

● useful advisory quotes from an acknowledged expert

● information about bereavement counselling services

● details of how to obtain financial help

● a book and leaflet list

● a list of useful addresses.

In the case of sudden avoidable death, details on how to recognise warning signs, preventative action and emergency first aid procedures should also be included.

Remember that the reason for writing an article is to inform the reader so even a subject as painfully personal as this one must contain relevant, up-to-date, factual information.

## USING PROFESSIONAL EXPERTISE

Taking the theme of writing about what you know one stage further, professional experts who can write with clarity about their subject are always in demand.

### Establishing street cred

Providing you have the relevant credentials, there are always openings for writers who can translate technical information into terms the layman can understand. In some cases, the expert's first attempts at article writing may be in response to a request from an editor seeking material. Listed below are just a few examples of the type of magazines where this may occur:

- 'alternative' health therapies
- financial
- collectibles
- insurance
- company 'in house'
- legal
- computer
- medical
- consumer
- scientific.
- electronic

All of the above examples cover areas where the professional in their field can find their expertise in demand.

### Cross-pollinating the markets

In a later chapter, we'll be looking at adapting your articles to suit different markets, and if you study the list above, it soon becomes clear that a writer who is also, say, an experienced lawyer need not confine themselves purely to legal publications.

Perhaps the lawyer has a passion for a particular make of car — Morris Minor or Volkswagen Beetle, for example. In addition to any features he or she may write about legal matters in general, there is also a clear possibility here for articles on a variety of law-related topics concerning car ownership and restoration. For example:

- your rights when buying and selling vehicles

- the law relating to roadworthiness

- the legal definition of 'vintage'
- laws governing the import and export of vehicles.

## SHARING HOBBIES AND INTERESTS

You may not be a qualified professional but you may, nevertheless, be an expert in your particular hobby. Indeed, sometimes the only difference between the gifted amateur and acknowledged professional is that the amateur is unpaid. Most enthusiasts subscribe to at least one magazine and many regularly write letters to the editor of their favourite publication.

Sharing hobbies and interests.

### Taking the next step up the ladder

Once you've had a few letters published, there is no reason why you should not take the next step and submit an article. However, before you submit any completed articles, it is essential that you study your chosen market carefully to establish the sort of feature they are likely to publish.

### Analysing the market

Whilst the articles described above would probably be most suitable for the smaller, specialist markets, some may also find a home in one of the many mainstream titles. Breaking into the major magazine market can be extremely difficult but fortunately, not impossible.

A quick scan of the listings in the *Writers' & Artists' Yearbook* (published by A & C Black) will reveal that few of the glossy monthlies are prepared to consider unsolicited manuscripts. Almost all of their material is either staff-written or commissioned from a pool of established freelances, usually well-known journalists or acknowledged experts in their particular fields.

### Diving into the pool

The situation with regard to women's weeklies and some of the smaller circulation specialist titles isn't quite so bad and currently, these offer

Magazine title ...........................................................................

Editor/editorial address................................................

......................................................................................

Cover price ............Weekly/monthly/quarterly/biannually/annually

| Content | Number of columns/page | Average number words per item | Staff-written* |
|---|---|---|---|
| Agony column | | | |
| Book/film/video reviews | | | |
| Celebrity interviews | | | |
| Competitions | | | |
| Crafts | | | |
| DIY | | | |
| Fashion | | | |
| Fiction | | | |
| Finance | | | |
| Food & drink | | | |
| Gardening | | | |
| Health & beauty | | | |
| Horoscopes | | | |
| Medical | | | |
| Motoring | | | |
| Patterns (knit/sew) | | | |
| Pets | | | |
| Readers' letters | | | |
| Readers' true life tales | | | |
| Special features | | | |
| Special offers | | | |
| The Arts | | | |
| Travel | | | |
| Other (specify) | | | |

TARGET GROUP.................................................................

Fig. 3. Magazine analysis sheet (women's magazines).

*Editorial staff are usually listed on either the first or last pages of the magazine.

some of the best opportunities for writers hoping to produce articles for the mass market readership.

If you intend to join the pool of established freelances, the first step is to choose a magazine which you particularly enjoy reading and analyse the format. Using Figure 3 as an example for the women's magazine market, you will find that a clear picture of the target readership will emerge. Whilst some of the categories will not apply, the analysis sheet can easily be adapted for specialist magazines.

Adrienne Wild, managing editor of gardening magazine *Gardening Answers*, is just one specialist magazine editor willing to consider illustrated articles from freelance contributors. She advises all would-be freelances to read the magazine before submitting completed manuscripts which must, of course, be written to the required length and style. Whilst Adrienne will send guidelines on receipt of an SAE, by applying the analysis sheet (Figure 3), experienced gardeners will gain a clear idea of the sort of article they should be writing for publication in the magazine.

Another specialist editor prepared to consider freelance submissions is John Lloyd of *Camping Magazine*. His comprehensive guidelines give details of his requirements for a range of features including equipment testing, travel, lifestyle and humour. He prefers would-be contributors to contact him first with their ideas and once again, the magazine analysis sheet applied in conjunction with his guidelines will provide a basis on which to draft your article outline.

## PRODUCING MATERIAL FOR NEWSPAPERS

News articles or 'stories' for newspapers are almost always written by staff journalists or professional freelances retained by the editor. It is, however, possible to write articles and occasional features for newspapers which have editorial space set aside for more general items. Some newspapers run occasional local interest features on topics such as:

● 'then and now' articles chronicling, for example, a lifetime working in local industry

● environmental and conservation projects

● historic buildings

● local history

● murders and haunted houses.

## BECOMING A REGULAR COLUMNIST

A one-off feature of this type could well lead to a regular column. You may be asked to deputise for an existing columnist writing in a similar field of expertise or your features may prove so popular that the editor decides to offer you a regular slot. In common with their magazine counterparts, many local newspapers carry some or all of the following editorial columns:

● agony

● astronomy

● children's page

● competitions

● cookery

● crossword

● DIY

● financial

● fishing

● gardening

● health

● legal

● motoring

● review (book, TV, film, CD, computer games, theatre, etc.)

● sport

● travel.

### Creating a niche

If the newspaper doesn't already have a column in your particular specialist field, it is always worth contacting the editor and suggesting that you write one for them. Bear in mind, however, that editorial space is at a premium in local newspapers and there simply may not be room for anything new.

In areas such as health, finance, gardening and DIY, short columns are often produced by major manufacturers in the various industries and circulated free of charge on a national basis.

As local newspaper budgets are very tight, an editor has to be convinced that paying you to produce a regular, personalised column is going to be more cost effective than reproducing one syndicated free to to the newspaper.

| Week No. | Deadline date | Publication date | Topic | Additional items | Wordcount |
|---|---|---|---|---|---|
| 1 | 19.12.9X | 2.1.9Y | Draftproofing your windows | Competitions – DIY quiz (closing date 12.1.9Y) | 500 + product shot of prize |
| 2 | 26.12.9X | 9.1.9Y | Insulating your loft | Manufacturer's list of protective measures | 500 + line drawings |
| 3 | 2.1.9Y | 16.1.9Y | Thawing frozen pipes | Manufacturer's safety instructions | 400 + photo |
| 4 | 9.1.9Y | 23.1.9Y | Clearing sink blockages | Step-by-step diagrams | 500 + line drawings |
| 5 | 16.1.9Y | 30.1.9Y | | Answers to quiz List of winners | |
| 6 | 23.1.9Y | 6.2.9Y | | DIY chain store Valentine promo. | product shot |
| 7 | 30.1.9Y | 13.2.9Y | Making a bird nesting box (Valentine theme) | | line drawings |

Fig. 4. Sample planner for weekly DIY column.

## Filling the space provided

Before you approach the editor, have in mind a clear format for your column and a list of topics to take you over a number of weeks. You will be allocated a set number of words and you will be expected to stick to this figure. Add interest by including 'fillers' in the form of diagrams, photographs and snippets from company press releases, cutting or expanding your articles accordingly to meet the required wordage. Details on how to obtain these are given in Chapter 10 but initially, information will filter through from publicity mass mail shots to the media or from eagle-eyed public relations companies who pick up your column through cuttings services.

You will be given a 'lead time', a weekly deadline which will probably be around a fortnight before the publication date. It is useful to make a chart along the lines of the sample for a weekly DIY column in Figure 4, showing when and where each item should appear. Seasons must be taken into account, so you need to plan well ahead to ensure the right piece appears at the right time, filling in any blanks as soon as material is available.

Assuming that the first issue (week number 1) is scheduled for the first week in January, a draftproofing article is ideal. The article will contain information on:

● the methods and products available

● preparation of surfaces

● the result you are aiming for.

A competition and photograph of the prize provides a filler for week 1, with the list of winners diaried forward for another filler for week 5.

### Stringing along

If you have a keen interest in local matters, you may be the ideal person to act as a **stringer** for your local newspaper. Having made yourself known to the editor through regular correspondence with the letters page or your own specialist column, he could ask you to become a 'stringer', keeping an eye out for any snippets of local news that you feel will be of interest and either writing them up yourself or passing them on to one of the staff journalists.

### Writing for national daily papers

Whilst it is by no means impossible to write for the national dailies, it can be very difficult for an unknown writer to obtain a commission. However, one of the best ways of getting your foot in the door is to build up a large portfolio of cuttings of your published work.

Once you have established a track record for reliability and subject expertise in the local press, a national newspaper editor may be prepared to consider an occasional one-off feature but be aware that you will be competing against a pool of very experienced professionals.

## CASE STUDIES

### Maureen tries her hand at travel writing

On her return from a thoroughly enjoyable package holiday in Greece, Maureen, a 30-year-old clerical worker, decides to write an article about her hilarious experiences at the hotel. Adding a word of warning about eating foreign food and family hotels full of shrieking children, she sends the article off to a women's magazine selected at random. It is returned with a standard rejection.

### Josie runs a marathon

Recently recovered from a potentially life-threatening illness, 54-year-old Josie, a grandmother of six, is preparing to take part in her very first marathon with the intention of raising money for the hospital unit that saved her life. She contacts the editor of a women's magazine aimed at the over-forties and they ask to see an outline of an article about her experiences. The editor commissions her to write the article, suggesting Josie waits until she has run the marathon so that she can describe her emotions on achieving her goal. The article, illustrated with photographs taken by a staff photographer, is published three months later in the magazine.

## CHECKLIST

1. Do you keep up to date with changes in your area of expertise?

2. Do you subscribe to a suitable trade journal?

3. Have you devised a forward planner for seasonal items?

4. Could you become a 'stringer' for your local newspaper?

5. Do you have additional skills you could apply to the content of the articles you write?

## ASSIGNMENT

Take a selection of magazines in your chosen field of interest and apply the magazine analysis in Figure 3 to each of them in turn. Comparison of the results will give you a clear overview of the target readerships and the differences in format and style between each publication.

# 4
# Researching and Filing Systems

## GATHERING INFORMATION

You can never have enough information about your chosen topic. Whether or not you are an expert in your own field, research is vital.

### Researching the subject

No matter how well you think you know your subject, there are always gaps somewhere in your personal knowledge.

It is a brave writer who makes factual statements without any source material to back them up. Failure to provide this can result in a flood of letters from irate readers and at worst, never working for that editor again.

Always check your facts with at least three different sources. Opinions vary, theories are disproved and it is not uncommon to discover that methods you have been applying successfully for years are now hopelessly out of date.

It is also surprising how often something we are sure is accurate is actually totally incorrect. Checking my sources paid off for me when I wanted to use a quote I believed was attributed to Mark Twain. A visit to my local library failed to unearth the quote, so I contacted the county library's literary expert. He could find no evidence that Mark Twain ever said it and worse still, the quote itself appeared not to exist. To this day, I still don't know where I got it from.

### Triple-checking your facts

Fortunately, rather than disproving a long-held belief like the one above, triple-checking your facts usually helps you to confirm that your information is correct.

Researching an article on Halloween superstitions for a magazine aimed at the younger women's market, I discovered a recipe for conjuring up an apparition of one's future husband. I'd never heard of the superstition before, so I scanned several reference books and to my delight, found it was well-documented in all of them. The end result was a fun piece with a slightly risqué flavour, reviving an ancient custom on love and marriage.

## Compiling a checklist

To ensure accuracy, before you complete the article, apply a checklist along the following lines:

● Have I made any statements which cannot be supported by a reputable source?

● Have I used the very latest information?

● Have I checked my facts against at least three sources?

● Have I double-checked all my figures and the wording of all my quotes?

● Are all quotes attributed to the correct sources?

Add your own checks to this list to ensure that the information contained in your articles is both current and accurate.

## GAINING ACCESS TO REFERENCE MATERIAL

### Joining a library

Enthusiasts invariably have extensive collections of books covering every aspect of their chosen field from coffee table volumes comprised of colour plates and little else, to complex technical manuals complete with blueprint diagrams.

However, no matter how many books we have on our specialist subject, there always comes a time when we need to track something down, cross reference or double-check our information, and the local library is an ideal source.

### Making friends with your librarian

Librarians have a vast amount of expertise and will give you invaluable help and advice on where to locate the information you require.

Where your local branch is unable to help, you will be referred to the relevant person or to a specialist reference library. Some reference libraries levy charges or membership fees and you may have to provide proof of your identity and purpose to gain access.

You can obtain more information on this and other reference societies and organisations from the *Aslib Directory of Information Sources in the UK* which you can find in your local library.

**Surfing the net**

If you are already on the Internet, you will know all about the vast store of information you can now access through your computer. Encyclopaedias, dictionaries and a wide variety of reference material are now available on CD Rom and for those who cannot access the World Wide Web at home, some central libraries are now on the Internet and the service is available free of charge.

## ESTABLISHING CONTACTS

The more articles you write, the more adept you will become at locating and gathering reference material.

You will soon build up a network of contacts who can provide you

with the information you require and, if necessary, pass you on to someone equally helpful. Ideally, you should be regarding each topic from a variety of angles so that, whilst one source will help you with one article, the next will lead you down another, equally lucrative path.

**Exploring unknown territory**

For example, perhaps you are writing an article on local buildings of unusual architectural interest. In the course of your research, you come across someone who tells you that one of the buildings has a resident ghost and introduces you to a local historian. You now discover that several of your chosen properties are said to be haunted and learn the stories behind them.

Now comes a further revelation – the historian has heard that there have been some strange supernatural incidents in the stockroom of a modern high street chemist shop. The pharmacist who suffered the experience agrees to see you and is, you discover in conversation, a soloist with the local choir.

You've never thought about the paranormal before or choral singing but a good article writer never wastes an opportunity and your research has led to you making a couple of very useful new contacts.

Beginning with your original idea, you now have several new opportunities for articles in different areas:

1. *TOPIC: Local buildings of architectural interest*
   (a) Architectural features.
   (b) The architects and planners behind each building.
   (c) The history of each building.
   (d) The background to each building and its influence on the area.
   (e) The occupants of each building.
   (f) The story of some of the individuals who occupied the buildings.

2. *TOPIC: Haunted buildings in the area and their ghosts*
   (a) Haunted modern buildings in the area.
   (b) The background and story of individual ghosts.
   (c) Other supernatural experiences in the locality.
   (d) Historical tales about influential inhabitants in previous centuries.

3. *TOPIC: The background to and future of the local choir*
   (a) Taking part in recitals and choral competitions.
   (b) Being a chorister, experience, training, what it entails, etc.
   (c) An interview with the choirmaster.
   (d) Humorous incidents in the life of a chorister.

### Knowing where to turn

The above examples are only a small sample of the articles which can mushroom from one basic idea.

As a bonus, not only do you have a variety of topics to write about, but you have also begun to establish a network of useful contacts. The advantages of knowing a local historian are obvious, but you also now have someone to turn to if you need technical advice not only on drugs and medicines but also on singing and music, in the shape of your spook-spotting, singing pharmacist.

### ATTENDING LECTURES AND CONFERENCES

Whether amateur enthusiast or professional expert, there is bound to be an organisation devoted entirely to your area of interest.

## Joining associations and societies

If you can, try to join at least one group and subscribe to at least one trade or specialist magazine. Many societies hold regular meetings and lectures and you should try to attend at least one a year. Where this is impossible, make sure you keep a close eye on any relevant literature that they send you. A well-organised group usually produces some form of newsletter or magazine which will keep you up to date with any changes, news and items of interest in your chosen area.

## Listening to lectures

Lectures and conferences offer an ideal opportunity to make new contacts and gather the very latest information. Attendance costs can range from as little as a couple of pounds for association members to a couple of hundred pounds for a residential conference. However, in terms of updating and extending your knowledge, it is money well spent and costs can be offset against tax.

## RECORDING AND STORING INFORMATION

Listed below are some minimum requirements for an article writer:

● various encyclopaedias and dictionaries

● a collection of both general and subject-specific reference books

● files of cuttings from newspapers, magazines, trade journals, etc.

● a notebook containing snippets of information (with the source and date noted)

● press release files

● magazine files

● a contact address book

● at least one directory of research sources

● a file of your own published articles.

## Using the right equipment

You will also need suitable equipment on which to produce your manuscripts. Initially, you may consider that writing a monthly newsletter for your club hardly warrants the purchase of a typewriter, let alone a personal computer, but this view can be very short-sighted.

A typewritten manuscript is much easier to set out for duplication, and more importantly, much easier to read. It also looks more professional and this will influence your approach to writing and make your article a more worthwhile proposition for the reader.

## WP OR PC?

Although some of the smaller press magazines request that you submit your manuscripts on computer disk, the mainstream market still tends to prefer the initial approach to be on paper. Once accepted, however, they will probably ask you to supply the piece on disk and it is simply not financially viable to pay someone to do this for you.

Later on, we'll be looking at the impact of modern technology on the freelance writer, but if you intend to produce articles on a regular basis you would be advised to invest in either a word processor (WP) or better still, a personal computer (PC), preferably with a combined modem and fax.

Anyone considering writing for the mass media should be aware that articles are already being submitted via E-Mail and it is only a matter of time before national publications will expect all their contributors to be on-line.

### Getting organised

For the computer literate, immediate transfer of every scribbled note of research and reference material onto suitably labelled floppy disks is the obvious step. For those who prefer a more traditional environment, sensibly labelled files are the answer. Whether electronic or manual, however, it is essential to devise a filing system that suits you.

For example, perhaps you write a DIY column. Initially, alphabetical order might seem the most obvious classification for filing your information, but as your files grow, things could become rather more complicated.

At first, it may seem sensible to file everything connected with, say, Wallpaper under the letter **W**. Therefore, information about Wall-stencilling would also be filed under **W**. OK so far, but where would you file additional stencilling information, about furniture or ceilings, for example? Under **S** for Stencils, **F** for Furniture, **C** for Ceilings or **W** with the instructions for stencilling Walls?

Before long, you will have to devise a system of cross-referencing, perhaps alphabetically, then by topic, then by method and so on.

### Accessing the information

Despite the growing use of computers, switching on, setting up and accessing the relevant program can be time-consuming. For the sake of speed, card indexes are still a very useful method of cataloguing and locating things quickly and there are advantages to be gained from having the information to hand on paper in a colour-coded, numbered file.

It is up to the individual writer to choose their preferred method, bearing in mind that the more comfortable you are with a system, the more organised and easier it will be to lay your hands on the information you require.

## UPDATING YOUR RECORDS

Try to keep your records as up to date as possible. People have a tendency to move on, so contact names and telephone numbers will change from time to time.

### Clearing out old material

Whenever possible, take the time to go through your files and clear out any obsolete material. Organisations are tending to revamp their images more frequently nowadays and societies have a habit of changing their names. New technology is also impacting in all kinds of ways, so regular clearouts are vital to avoid confusion. Do take care, however, not to destroy anything that might turn out to be useful. If in doubt, rather than throw it out, the wary article writer will hang onto it, however dubious it might be.

## CASE STUDIES

### Bill gets egg on his face

Bill's local history article has been published in his parish magazine. The piece concerns the background to an area of common land, known locally as 'Drake's Run'. Basing his article on an old folktale his gran told him about the land being named after Sir Francis Drake, Bill fails to check his facts. Shortly after the article is published, the local vicar receives dozens of letters from his parishioners informing him that the name originated from the now defunct practice of driving flocks of ducks across the land to market.

### Terry sets up a system

Having sold several articles to specialist magazines, Terry, a retired accountant, sets up a system of cross-referencing, storage and retrieval on his personal computer and compiles a list of suitable markets for articles, detailing the editorial requirements for each individual magazine. He now has easy access to accurate information for a variety of articles and markets.

## CHECKLIST

1. Do you have a filing system in place?

2. Are your files clearly labelled?

3. Are you a member of a professional/trade association?

4. Do you have a supply of reference books?

5. Do you have your own personal directory of contacts?

## ASSIGNMENT

Select a topic and write down as many facts about it off the top of your head as you can. Now check each fact in turn from the information you have in your home. Did you get your facts right? If the answer is 'no', do not attempt to write an article until you have updated all the relevant information. If 'yes', did you discover anything new you could add to your article?

Do you have a filing system in place?

# 5
# Rewriting to Suit Different Markets

One of the advantages of article writing is that the same information can be utilised again and again, providing it is written to the editorial style of each individual publication.

## ADAPTING YOUR STYLE

Depending on the slot you are writing for, there may also be scope to vary your style to suit the topic you are writing about. For example, the following extracts are taken from two articles I wrote for a newspaper column I produced for teenagers.

*Extract 1*

If you need some extra cash to see you through further education courses, it's not too difficult to find yourself a summer job. Depending on your age and qualifications, there is a wealth of opportunity to not only earn money but also gain experience for your future career.

*Extract 2*

My sister had done it again. She'd been over my things without asking permission and had borrowed the black skirt I wanted to wear for a special date. I stormed into her room in a fury, 'I'll give you five seconds to give me back my skirt,' I shook my fist at the relaxed figure lying on the bed, 'or I won't be responsible for my actions.'

The first example is purely factual, setting out holiday job opportunities for students. The second, whilst it is factually accurate, is a light-hearted approach to coping with stress.

### Respecting the reader

When I was asked to write the column, I knew how important it was not to patronise my teenage readers.

With straight information pieces like the student holiday one, I stuck to a standard factual format, but for others, I decided that the best way to achieve reader identification was to invent a younger sister who would invariably get the better of me.

By the end of the two years in which I produced the column, I had created a complete cast of fictional characters to portray the factual situations I wrote about each week. Through the story-telling quality provided by the dialogue and interaction between the characters, I was able to tackle topics as serious as drug-taking without preaching or talking down to my readership.

## Wearing different hats

You should be prepared to change your writing style to suit not only the topics you are covering but also the readership of each individual publication.

Read the magazines and newspapers you intend to write for and get to know their formats inside out. Subscribe to them for several months and try to absorb the style and feel of the editorial and feature articles.

Take a simple theme and write a paragraph about it. The example below tackles hygiene in the kitchen, beginning by explaining the correct method of washing your hands before preparing food.

Before you touch any food, wash your hands thoroughly. Fill the sink with water. Take a bar of soap and with your hands in the water rub the soap in between your palms to work up a lather. Make sure you clean in between your fingers and use a nailbrush to scrub any dirt from under your nails. When you have finished, rinse off the soap and dry your hands on a clean towel.

Now rewrite this or your own passage in the editorial style of any one or all of the following publications:

- a magazine aimed at young, single women

- a magazine aimed at mature women

- a cookery magazine

- a food industry leaflet

- a handbook for canteen staff

- a children's cookery column

- your local newspaper

- a quality national newspaper

- a tabloid newspaper

- a humorous, personal experience article.

## ALTERING THE ANGLE

Different markets demand a different approach, so you will have to adapt the format accordingly.

### Knowing where to put the emphasis

Returning to the above list, a leaflet for the food industry would probably take the form of a step-by-step guide to cleanliness in the kitchen. For a tabloid newspaper, the handwashing part of the article would be a tiny section in a shock piece on poor hygiene in the average home.

Whilst both articles would tackle the link between unwashed hands and food contamination, in the industry leaflet the emphasis would be on the correct procedure to minimise the chance of infection. In the tabloid piece, the emphasis would be on true life horror stories of people contracting life-threatening illnesses from eating contaminated food.

## MAKING THEM LAUGH

Humour is a very powerful tool in getting a message over to a reader. Everyone enjoys a good laugh and a piece describing the disastrous attempts of the writer to achieve their goal can not only entertain but also inform.

### Laughing at yourself

Unfortunately, it is extremely difficult to make people laugh and unless it comes naturally to you, it is best avoided. However, well-written humour hugely increases your chances of a sale so providing you have the ability to laugh at yourself, you may strike gold. When writing humour, bear in mind the following points:

● The reader must be able to identify with the situation you are describing.

● You must have an empathy with the reader.

● Avoid making fun of anyone but yourself.

● Use the word 'you' as much as possible.

● Be prepared to be the 'fall guy', making yourself the butt of any jokes.

● Never appear so stupid that the reader will be contemptuous of you.

● Take the 'everyman' role, so that you establish an immediate link with the reader.

Your aim is to have the reader laughing with, not at, you. They should be able to immediately recognise the people and situations you are describing and relate to your situation sympathetically.

## Sending up familiar situations

When writing for a specialist market, you have the advantage of being able to use so-called 'in-house' humour. This is where you are writing about a profession, hobby or lifestyle that you share with your readership. You could for example, write humorous pieces on your disastrous first attempts in any of the following fields:

● amateur photography

● camping

● DIY

● oil painting

● sailing

● sport

and so on. Many of your readers will have made similar mistakes to the ones you are describing and an instant empathy will be established between you.

Alternatively you may be writing for a national market, where your readers would relate to day-to-day situations such as:

● assembling a flatpacked piece of furniture

● high street shopping with a double-buggy

● holiday packing for a family of four

● how to survive building an extension to your house.

## Laughing at work and play

One of the advantages of writing for publications such as your club or firm's magazine, is that you have immediate reader identification with the situations and events you are describing. Your readers will already have a rapport with you and it will be much easier to make them laugh about situations in which they have been personally involved.

## TAKING PHOTOGRAPHS

Photographs not only offer a visual dimension to your articles but may also attract an extra fee. Black and white photographs are still widely used, although colour transparencies are usually acceptable. Take several pictures of your subject from a variety of angles and select the ones that best illustrate the piece you are writing.

## Developing your film

No matter how fond you are of your battered old Brownie, if you intend to submit photographs to illustrate your article, use a good camera. Modern cameras do almost all the focusing and winding on for you, so there is no excuse for submitting photos with fuzzy images or double exposures.

You will need to use a specialist photography shop to develop your black and white film. Ask for a 'contact sheet' – your set of photographs printed on one sheet – from which you can select the clearest and most effective prints.

## Employing professional photographers

Many magazines employ their own staff photographers or commission freelances to illustrate your article for you.

*Bella*, for example, send along their own photographer to take the pictures of the people and homes which accompany their 'true-life' features.

In some cases, you may have a professional contact of your own whom you can suggest to an editor, although you will lose out on any fee for illustrations.

You can also obtain photographs from picture libraries but you will have to pay for this service. Fortunately, photographs and colour slides that arrive attached to press releases are intended for publication and you can use these free of charge. PR companies will, however, expect you to return transparencies after use.

## Captioning and cross-referencing photographs

Every photograph you submit will need a caption and you must make it clear to the editor exactly which section of the text it refers to. Perhaps the simplest method is to number each photograph, annotating your manuscript accordingly as shown in Figure 5.

## Fixing the captions

Put your name, address and telephone number on the back of the photograph either lightly in pencil or preferably printed on a small adhesive label. Never write in ink as this will show through and can spoil the surface.

Numbered captions should be typed on adhesive labels and fixed to the back of the relevant photo. For colour slides, place each transparency inside an envelope with the caption typed on it.

Fig. 5. Photograph of Lavenham Church, Suffolk.

*(reproduced courtesy of Linda Sutton)*

Annotate photographs within the text of your article, numbering them consecutively for easy identification, e.g. '. . . *our tour of the area ended with a visit to Lavenham Church (Pic 3). This superb example of . . . '*

## Brushing up your camera techniques

Because photographs often attract an extra fee, it is worth brushing up on your camera technique and ensuring that you supply good, clear photographs.

The copyright in a photograph belongs, initially, to the person who takes the picture, so in theory, they can be used again and again. However, if you intend to rewrite your article for several different markets, bear in mind that the pictures must be tailored to suit the various formats. Photographs should be:

● numbered and have captions which relate to the text

● sharp and clear

● trimmed to fit the allotted space

● well-balanced so that the subject is clearly framed by the background.

Copyright in any photographs you take should remain with you so you must ensure that you are informed in writing of the copyright you have sold and whether or not you are at liberty to sell the photograph on elsewhere.

## QUOTING THE EXPERTS

There is no copyright on fact, only in the form of words that is used. If, for example, I state that any change in your life, no matter whether it is good or bad, will cause you some inconvenience, this could be said to be a statement of fact.

Alternatively, I could use the following quote, 'Change is not made without inconvenience, even from worse to better,' Samuel Johnson (*A Dictionary of the English Language*).

Scanning the page, you can see the difference in the way that the two statements are laid out. The first is indistinguishable from the body of the text, the other is set within speech marks and credited to the person who first said it.

### Crediting your source

You should always state the source of any quotations that you use. When writing instructional articles, you will need to refer to and quote from standard textbooks in order to establish credibility and subject matter.

In more light-hearted articles, you may wish to use well-known quotations to illustrate your point. In both cases, you should double-check the wording in order to avoid misquoting the source.

### Infringing copyright

According to the *Writers' & Artists' Yearbook* (A & C Black), you can 'quote up to 200 words for the purpose of criticism or review'. For any other purpose or larger sections, you should seek permission from the publisher of the work.

However, even for very short passages, crediting the source of a quotation not only reinforces your subject expertise to the reader but is also a matter of common courtesy to your fellow professionals. Treat them courteously in the first instance and they will be only too pleased to give you further help whenever the need arises.

## CONDUCTING INTERVIEWS

A good interviewer is a person who is outgoing, friendly and genuinely enjoys meeting new people.

### Who do you interview?

As far as the media is concerned, the ideal interviewee is someone everyone wants to read about. The sole survivor of a major air disaster, the victor in a multi-million pound libel action, the spouse of a tragic murder victim.

However, the people involved in these and similar national news items will invariably be inaccessible to the average freelance writer. Those who decline to sign immediately an exclusive contract with a national newspaper, magazine or publicist will usually be snapped up by professional journalists working for international news agencies. The interviews will be syndicated to the media in the UK and abroad until interest wanes and the income runs dry.

There is, nevertheless, plenty of opportunity for you to place well-written interviews with people likely to be of interest to a specific readership, providing the content is topical.

## Looking for an angle

If you intend to write celebrity interviews for publication, then you must be aware of the media's attitude towards them. Providing your interviewee is currently in the public eye, your interview will be saleable. If not, then no matter how famous they used to be, no editor will be interested in publishing the piece.

Whether or not your subject is in the public eye, an interview is rarely solely about the interviewee. It also serves to inform the reader about a particular item of interest. In order to catch the eye of an editor, the people you interview should be currently engaged in a new project. They may, for example:

● have just written a book, or made a record, TV programme or film

● have invented a revolutionary new process

● be in the process of achieving success in an area entirely new to them

● be the first or last person to have been involved in an event of current national interest.

## Hanging it on a hook

Where you are featuring professional experts, rather than well-known media personalities, you need to find a 'hook' on which to hang your article. For example, for an interview aimed at a magazine for photography enthusiasts, the interviewee could be:

● a photographer (amateur or professional) who captured an historic incident on film

● a person who devised a revolutionary innovation in camera design

● a photographer (amateur or professional) who produces specialist pictures – nature, portraits, wide-angled, sport, etc.

An interview featuring any of the above subjects is unlikely to stand on its own. In order to make it publishable, it will have to be linked with a current event. The anniversary of the historic incident, for example, or a much improved version of the camera's design change, or an exhibition of the photographer's work.

Keep an eye out for anniversaries. People who were in on the beginning of a brand new process or invention planning to celebrate its twenty-fifth year in commercial use are ideal for this purpose. Always look for an angle and seek out ordinary people who have done extraordinary things.

## Preparing beforehand

In order to conduct a successful interview, you must be prepared by ensuring that you have all of the following:

● prior knowledge of the interviewee and their area of expertise

● a prepared list of questions

● an appointment

● the ability to listen.

## Asking the right questions

The questions you ask will depend very much on the type of article you are writing. If it is aimed at a women's magazine, then the emphasis will be on the person's background, home and family.

If it is for a specialist hobby or professional publication, the emphasis will be on subject expertise. As a rough guide, a good interview should contain:

● a brief physical description of the interviewee

● a brief description of your surroundings

● factual information about the person's area of expertise

● some background information about the person

● a little about how they envisage their future or the development of their project

● a list of useful addresses where you can obtain further information.

An optional extra is a photograph of the person, their surroundings and/or workplace and/or the equipment they use.

## Having a friendly chat

It pays to let the interviewee do all the talking. The more you take the role of fascinated listener, the more they will tell you about themselves. Try to avoid asking **closed** questions. These are questions to which the answer can only be either 'yes' or 'no'. For example:

● Do you enjoy your job?

● Is the equipment complicated to use?

● Are you planning to marry in the foreseeable future?

Faced with a shy or, indeed, hardened interviewee, the above questions will be useless in obtaining the replies you are after. Always ask **open** questions, ones that will encourage your interviewees to talk about themselves:

● What is it about your job that gives you most satisfaction?

● The equipment looks rather complicated. How can a layman use it?

● You've been with your partner for some time now. How do you see your future together?

## Listing dates and checking your facts

List any dates you are given and double-check them before you leave. You may prefer to make a recording of the conversation but be aware that many people find having their conversation taped intrusive and possibly intimidating.

If you genuinely find it difficult to make comprehensive notes during the interview, ask permission to tape it. Use a machine with a built-in microphone as this is less intrusive and you avoid problems with setting it up correctly.

Some interviewees will have press photos you can use to accompany the article. If not, ask before you take photographs – never just snap away without permission.

## Being trustworthy

It is vital that you prove you can be trusted. If your interviewee has confided in you, don't break their confidence or they will spread the word and you'll find other people will be reluctant to speak to you.

If the interviewee made you welcome, write and thank them for their hospitality and always check your copy with them before submitting it to the editor. Sensational 'inside stories' are best left to the tabloid journalists. If you want to write regularly for the less controversial markets, build up a reputation of trust and accuracy and you will find yourself in great demand.

## Interviewing styles

Interviews are conducted and written-up in a variety of styles, depending upon the preference of the writer and the format of the magazine. An interview may be:

- straightforward question and answer (Q & A)

- a cosy chat using direct speech

- an article on a specific topic, using snatches of Q & A dialogue to explain technical information

- a representation of the interviewee as seen through the eyes of the interviewer

- a comparison of three different people's experiences, one good, one bad, one balancing the other two.

## Giving the reader what they want

A good interview is one in which the questions elicit the answers everyone, i.e. your readers, want to hear. Experienced interviewees will be skilled in avoiding revealing the things they don't want you to know. Inexperienced subjects may have difficulty giving you the answers you require. It is up to you to ask the right questions and interpret the answers correctly and in a manner that will inform and hold the reader through to the end.

## CASE STUDIES

### Pam goes back to school

Pam, a keen letter writer to magazines and newspapers, learns that one of her neighbours was the last headteacher of the long-closed village school. She conducts a lengthy interview with her and sends it to the editor of her local newspaper. It is returned with a brief note explaining that as the school closed so long ago, the interview has no topical interest for their readers.

### Sandra finds a hook

Sandra, a member of a writers' circle, is collecting her child benefit at the post office when she sees an actor from a now-defunct television series. Eavesdropping on the conversation with the counter clerk, Sandra discovers that the actor is an expert cactus grower who has taken time out from acting to write a book on his horticultural activities. He is happy to give her an interview, which she sells to the local newspaper to appear in time to coincide with the publication of his book.

## CHECKLIST

1.  Can you rewrite your article to suit several different markets?

2.  Are all quotes credited to the correct sources?

3.  Is your article topical?

4.  Will the humour appeal to a sufficiently wide readership?

5.  Is your interview with someone currently in the public eye?

## ASSIGNMENT

Choose someone, either alive or dead, whom you would love to interview and compile a list of questions you would like to ask them. Ask a friend to assume the role of interviewee and see if your questions elicit the answers you expected.

Is your article topical?

# 6
# Writing Short Stories

## UNDERSTANDING THE MARKET

In the previous chapters, we looked at the disciplines involved in writing factual articles for publication.

For many would-be fiction writers, keen to see their literary masterpieces in print, it can be quite a shock to discover that not only do exactly the same disciplines apply but that there are far fewer openings for short stories than there are for non-fiction articles.

### Defining the short story

A short story may be defined as a work of fiction not exceeding 10,000 words in length. However, the market for 10,000-word stories is so limited as to be almost non-existent. The best hope of seeing your stories in print is to aim them at specific magazines which you know publish the sort of story you enjoy writing.

The market for short stories falls into two main categories:

1. genre publications, i.e. Horror, Fantasy, Science Fiction (SF), Crime and Romance

2. women's magazines.

There are also a number of literary outlets which will consider fiction from new writers.

### Getting paid for your stories

As far as genre publications are concerned, the good news is that they may be willing to publish much longer stories than those featured in women's magazines. Some might even accept stories of up to and over 8,000 words.

The bad news is that payment rates are often very low and in some cases, non-existent.

### Playing fair with the writer

This is not a deliberate attempt to defraud the writer, simply a question of basic economics.

Magazine production costs are relatively high and editors have to economise somewhere. A large proportion of genre magazines are produced by small presses, fan clubs and writers' groups or are imported from overseas. They may be available only on subscription and have fairly low circulation figures. Reputable editors will do their best to pay their contributors a basic fee and should profits begin to rise, will try to increase payment rates accordingly.

Providing you find an editor who will play fair with you, these markets can offer a reputable route to publication for a host of budding genre fiction authors.

The same is true of literary publications, many of which are produced by legitimate writing organisations. In common with the genre magazines, whilst financial rewards may be scant, the good ones offer a useful showcase for new writing talent.

Literary short stories also feature in some national newspapers although, like *The Mail on Sunday's YOU* magazine, which publishes romance and twist-in-the-tale stories, their fiction is invariably commissioned from established, published authors.

Perhaps the best known media outlet for literary short stories is the fifteen-minute daily BBC Radio 4 slot. Although most of the stories are commissioned, unsolicited manuscripts from unpublished authors are considered.

## Steering clear of vanity publishers

When scanning national newspapers for possible markets, steer well clear of any advertisements offering publication of your short stories in an anthology. These are nothing more than con tricks on the part of greedy vanity publishers and work along the same lines as their better-publicised counterparts operating in the poetry world.

Readers are invited to submit their stories, often as competition entries. They then receive a letter singing their praises with the promise of publication in the next edition of the publisher's anthology. The author is subsequently invited to purchase the anthology for a knockdown price and, inspired by success, is usually unable to resist the temptation to order not just one but several more copies to distribute among family and friends.

Sadly, this will be just about as wide as the distribution network gets. Volumes produced by the vanity press are invariably poorly produced and unsaleable to reputable retail outlets.

It is, in fact, incredibly difficult to get an anthology of short stories accepted for publication by a genuine publishing house. The few that are published are designed to fit into set categories and of these, the majority are collections of stories by several well-known authors in a specific field – horror, crime or ghost stories, for example, preferably by long-dead authors whose works are out of copyright and therefore economical to reprint.

A small number of anthologies feature stories by one highly saleable author on a set theme, and other selections can be found in specialist areas such as gay or lesbian fiction, ethnic stories and feminist issues.

For writers tempted by dreams of stardom to part with their hard-earned cash, the following rule applies equally to poetry, autobiographies, novels and short stories:

---

**PUBLISHERS PAY YOU**

---

Treat any advertisements offering to publish an anthology of your work with extreme caution, and if anyone asks you for money, grab your manuscripts and run as fast as you can in the opposite direction.

## Writing for women's magazines

For those authors who wish to write short fiction for the mass market, women's weekly magazines are almost the only outlet accessible to them.

Whilst there are one or two fiction opportunities in women's monthly magazines, they are limited. The bulk of the material featured in the monthlies is staff-written, commissioned from well-known authors or extracts from serialisations of published novels.

The fiction pages of women's weeklies are more accessible to freelance contributors than their monthly counterparts. The stories may have few literary pretentions but they nevertheless entertain millions of readers every week. Fees vary across the industry but you are not expected to produce material without payment and you will have the satisfaction of seeing your work regularly on sale in newsagents nationwide.

## ANALYSING PUBLISHED FICTION

The one thing you cannot do if you want to see your fiction published in a women's magazine is send the editor any story of any length, style or genre you choose.

### Knowing who publishes what

Each magazine has its own format, tone, style and target readership. Before you send your manuscript off, you must know you are aiming it in the right direction.

Choose a selection of magazines which you enjoy reading and study them from cover to cover. There will usually be a note on an editorial page

Magazine ..........................................................................

Fiction editor* ...............................................................

Editorial address ...........................................................

..........................................................................

..........................................Tel: ......................

..........................................................................

**Type of fiction**                **No. of words**

Romance                             ........................

Lifestyle                           ........................

Twist-in-the-tale                   ........................

Serial                              ........................

Other (specify)                     ........................

Approx. age of characters ...........................................

Occupations .................................................................

Theme of story ...........................................................

Vocabulary (formal, slang, etc.) ...............................

Style (gentle, tough, etc.) ........................................

Fig. 6. Story analysis form.
*Editorial staff are usually listed either on the first or last pages of the magazine.

either at the beginning or at the end of the magazine, stating whether or not the editor is prepared to consider stories submitted 'on spec'.

Please heed warnings stating that 'we do not consider unsolicited manuscripts'. Ignoring them is pointless and in order to push this point home, some editors add a further deterrent in the form of a disclaimer concerning the safe return of unsolicited material.

If there is no indication in the magazine, check in the *Writers' & Artists' Yearbook* or telephone the magazine's editorial department to ask whether they are prepared to read stories submitted 'on spec' and to establish the name of the fiction editor.

Use the magazine analysis sheet (Figure 3) to determine the format, tone and target readership of your chosen publications, then apply the story analysis form in Figure 6 to the fiction in each magazine.

From your research, you will discover that the proportion of fiction varies enormously from one magazine to another.

## The changing face of fiction

Most feature only one very short story, between 850 and 1,200 words and often with a surprise or twist ending. Others have as many as three or four complete stories and a romantic serial, but these are the exception rather than the rule.

If you are one of the many writers who cut your teeth on the short stories in your mother or grandmother's weekly magazines, reading a current issue of *Woman* or *Woman's Own* can be something of a culture shock. Over the past ten years or so, the influence of the German publishing industry on the UK market has made a profound difference to the format and style of women's weeklies.

The introduction of titles such as *Bella* and *Best* in the 1980s took the industry by storm and opened the way for others in their mould. Meanwhile, in an effort to combat falling circulation figures as their readership transferred its affections to the new style magazines, old faithfuls such as *Woman* and *Woman's Own* began to update their image.

As a result, the tone, format and length of magazine fiction has changed dramatically from the days when you had at least one complete romantic story and a serial to get your teeth into each week.

## RELATING TO THE READERSHIP

In order to understand why the German magazines knocked their UK counterparts off their perches, you need to be aware of who actually reads the stories you wish to write.

## Looking at their faces

One of the advantages of the new style magazines is the number of 'true-life tales' they feature, accompanied by photographs of the people involved.

Look at their faces, study the articles and familiarise yourself with their lifestyles. Perhaps the most notable changes have been in the attitude towards single and working mothers.

A large proportion of the women featured are lone parents, and as so many mothers go out to work, the pace at which they live their lives has increased enormously. Stay-at-home mums preoccupied with housework, cooking and child-rearing are no longer the target readership.

For todays's modern reader, cleaning the house is a necessary evil, convenience foods are the norm and their children attend playgroups or nurseries, or are cared for by childminders.

Look closely too at the differences between age and social groups. In a magazine like *That's Life* aimed at younger women, the vocabulary, attitudes and behaviour will be very different from that reflected in *Woman's Realm*, which is designed to appeal to the over-forties.

## Paying attention to the advertisements

Study the advertisements in your chosen publications. What sort of products are they selling?

Look, too, at the cookery, fashion, beauty and health pages. You will find that, in magazines aimed primarily at young mums, many of the products featured are linked to leading catalogue companies and major chain stores.

For older readers, the emphasis is on health products, stair lifts, support hose and foot warmers.

## Empathising with the reader

If, when you read the magazine, you find that you cannot relate to the characters in the stories or the people in the true-life features, try another market for your work.

You will not, through your fiction, make your readers rethink their attitudes, bring them to a higher intellectual plane or encourage them to be interested in people whose lives have no relevance whatsoever to their own.

Magazine short stories are 'quick-fix' entertainment. If you would really like to give it a try but are not quite sure whether a particular magazine is right for you, a glance through the letters pages should clinch it for you.

## Sharing experiences

The letters will contain anecdotes, family stories, tips and comments which you instantly recognise and hopefully relate to. They might cover any or a mixture of the following:

● an amusing story about a grandchild

● a complaint about lack of facilities in shops for mums with pushchairs

● a middle-aged mother's thwarted attempt to return to the workplace

● retraining after redundancy

● the hopelessness of being a young jobless person

- an account of an amusing incident at home or in the workplace
- the joys of being a parent
- a gripe about rude shop assistants or offensive customers.

The subjects chosen will give you a clear indication of the age range of your readership, the things that interest them and the vocabulary they use.

## Writing about real people

Whichever publications you attempt to write for, you must write about people to whom the readership can relate. They must be instantly recognisable and, within the confines of your fictional story, the backgrounds, settings and situations must be as real as you can possibly make them.

Magazine fiction is character-driven, which means that the emphasis must be on the characters rather than the settings, which should simply serve to enhance the characterisation.

## Escaping into make-believe

The amount of truly escapist fiction in women's magazines is surprisingly small. There are one or two publications which still feature traditional 'boy meets girl' and historical romances, but these are the exception.

In the main, modern magazines are looking for modern attitudes and situations in their storylines. The story's characters must reflect the age range of the readership and the relationships must reflect today's society, whether the story involves coping with early retirement or having your central character agonising over whether she should commit herself to marriage with her long-term lover.

## EXPLORING YOUR OPTIONS

The type of story you write will depend on what gives you the most pleasure and the format of the magazine at which you are aiming your manuscripts.

Sending a tough twist-ender to a magazine which you know only publishes gentle romance is a total waste of effort. Get to know your chosen markets inside out over a period of months, until you reach the point when you can be reasonably confident that your story does fit into the right fiction category.

## Categorising short stories

Remember that modern readers live hectic lives. Magazine stories tend to be categorised under titles such as:

- 3 Minute Fiction

● Quick Read

● Coffee Break Fiction

● Story on a Page.

One magazine, which used to describe its stories as 'heartwarming', 'sensitive' and 'moving', now simply publishes fiction under the heading 'short story'. This alone demonstrates the change in emphasis for today's busy reader.

As detailed in the story analysis form, there are four main types of magazine fiction:

1. Romance

2. Twist-in-the-tale

3. Lifestyle

4. Serials.

Romances are tales of love and hope for the future. They may not be quite the standard 'boy meets girl' format but the characters do fall in love and for the most part, there is the promise that they will live happily ever after.

## Twist/surprise endings

Stories with a twist or surprise ending, originally rather hard-edged when introduced by the German magazines almost ten years ago, have been gradually softening in response to the need of the readership for uplifting stories which, for a brief moment, will take them away from the less pleasant aspects of their daily lives.

The advantage of the twist-in-the-tale format is that the stories fall into almost any genre, from romance to murder mystery. *Bella* magazine will even consider science fiction twists providing they fit the magazine's format, offering a lone outlet for this specialised genre within the women's magazine market.

## Coping with everyday situations

Lifestyle stories have, in some cases, replaced the standard romance. In these stories, the characters deal with the sort of problems that the readership will understand and immediately relate to. Topics such as:

● taking a long, hard look at their marriage

● struggling with the role of step-parent

● overcoming a teenage child's hostility

● rebuilding life after a broken romance

● forming relationships as the parent of a disabled child

● rethinking attitudes within a relationship and meeting others
  halfway

● facing and coping with a new way of life.

## Serialising your story

Magazines like *Woman's Weekly* and *My Weekly* do still take serials,
although a large proportion are adaptations of published novels.
There is, nevertheless, always room for a good writer who can break
their stories down into bite-sized chunks that will appeal to the magazine's readership. Serials also form one of the few categories in which
historical romance still features.

## Fitting into other categories

In order to have the best chance of acceptance, the wise fiction writer
will produce stories with a specific magazine slot in mind.

However, every now and then, a new opportunity arises and you may
just be lucky enough to be in the right place at the right time. Whilst it
is extremely rare for an editor to be so taken with a manuscript that falls
outside their usual format that it will be accepted for publication, the
inspired opportunist can occasionally strike lucky.

## Hitting the holiday season

It is not unusual for a major magazine to bring out a Summer or Winter
special or a 'library' edition – a collection of stories previously published in the magazine. At Christmas time, a magazine may also bring
out a double-issue to take them over the holiday period.

There are also certain times of the year, particularly during holiday
seasons, when editors can find themselves short of material to fill their
pages. It is at these times when they may be prepared to consider using
a longer piece than usual or something with a slightly different slant.

## Taking something from the 'slush' pile

It is very rare indeed for this type of fiction to be taken from the stack
of unsolicited manuscripts, commonly referred to as the 'slush' pile, that
clutter the desks of all magazine fiction editors. Editors seeking something new or stories to make up a special edition will usually make direct
contact with writers with a proven track record to ask if they can provide
them with anything suitable. Such an approach from an editor should

never be seen as a commission. A commissioned piece is one where there is a written agreement regarding format and payment between the editor and the writer before a manuscript is produced.

A telephoned request for sample stories is only one stage up from sending your work 'on spec'. The editor is quite entitled to return your manuscripts as unsuitable and you have to take that decision on the chin. The fact that you were approached at all is an excellent sign that the editor has faith in your ability and is keen to use your work.

## FOLLOWING THE GUIDELINES

We'll be looking at lengths and formats for the above magazine fiction categories in Chapter 8, but by far the best way to find out what they want is to read the magazines and familiarise yourself with the type of stories they publish.

Editors who are prepared to consider unsolicited manuscripts will usually issue editorial guidelines which will give you an idea of the sort of thing they are looking for. However, be aware that these are only a guide. They will not tell you how to write the stories and they are regularly updated. When you send off for guidelines, remember to include a stamped self-addressed envelope or you will not receive a reply.

### Giving the editors what they want

The feedback writers get from individual editors varies enormously depending on their personalities. Some have a reputation for being exceptionally kind and supportive, others less so, but they all have one thing in common. Despite appearances to the contrary, they would all genuinely like to be able to publish your work.

If, therefore, they take the trouble to send you editorial guidelines, study them carefully to ensure that the manuscripts you submit fit the brief you have been given as closely as possible.

### Reading the magazine

There is no doubt that nothing irritates an editor more than receiving manuscripts from writers who have clearly never read their magazine. Almost all editorial guidelines urge would-be contributors to read the publication over a lengthy period before submitting any manuscripts. As stated above, magazines revamp on a regular basis, so you really need to study the format over several months.

### Duplicating ideas

Reading the stories each week not only gives you an idea of the type of characters, themes and settings you should feature, but also stops you duplicating storylines. One of the commonest reasons for rejection is that your story is just too similar to one already accepted for publication. Jane Weatherall, editor of *Yours*, a magazine aimed primarily at the mature reader, lists the following themes to avoid:

● death

● illness

● too much infirmity

● violence

● old people going into old people's homes

● old people mourning the death of their spouses and then finding a new love at a tea dance/bowls club/library/old people's home.

### Giving you a hint

Editors are always on the lookout for regular contributors. When they receive a manuscript for publication, they can tell very quickly whether the author is likely to repeat their success or whether this story is a one-off lucky fluke.

Once published in a particular magazine, you stand a better chance of having more accepted by the same editor. By the time you have had several stories published, you should have built up a rapport with the editor and it is at this stage in your relationship that you may be asked to produce something new.

Now is the time to seize the opportunity to ask them exactly what they are looking for in the fiction you send them. Whilst the answers you receive may not be as enlightening as you had hoped, you will at least gain an insight into what you are up against. When you tentatively suggest a storyline, the response will probably be something along the following lines:

● 'Not sure, send me a draft and I'll cast my eye over it.'

● 'I've never tried that before, write it up and see how it turns out.'

● 'Sounds OK, let me have a look at it sometime.'

● 'I'm not sure what I want exactly, but I'll know it when I see it.'

That last statement is my favourite and the editor who made it will almost certainly recognise herself, as will her regular contributors.

Similar responses will also be given when you are past the awful stage of receiving standard rejection slips and as a reward for your patient perseverance in the face of adversity, are offered a crumb of explanation when your manuscript is returned.

Editors work under enormous pressure and it really isn't possible for them to give every contributor a blow-by-blow résumé of why their manuscript was unsuitable. The best you can hope for, apart from, 'this would be fine if you could just cut out all the characters and change the beginning, middle and end,' is something along the following lines:

● 'I'm afraid this isn't suitable for our magazine.'

● 'This doesn't quite work.'

● 'We no longer take stories on this theme.'

● 'This is too sharp/soft/complicated/slow/fast . . . etc. for our readers.'

It is an accepted truth among fiction writers that the stories you are sure are absolutely perfect for a particular magazine will invariably be rejected whilst the ones you are a little nervous about are, more often than not, accepted.

It is, therefore, best to write about characters and themes that interest you for magazines you enjoy reading. By having fun with your writing and producing stories for readers with whom you have an empathy, you will not only increase your own personal satisfaction but also your chances of having your stories accepted for publication.

## CASE STUDIES

### Elizabeth writes a romance
Elizabeth is an English graduate in her early thirties. She never reads women's magazines but is sure that the stories must be very simple to write. Having made the assumption that the sort of person who enjoys reading magazine fiction will be looking for escapism, she writes a 10,000 word story about a young heiress to a country estate, who falls in love with the stable lad. She sends it to *Woman* magazine because she remembers her mother reading it some twenty years ago. It is returned with a standard rejection slip.

### Carol faces reality
Although Carol's children are still in their early teens, they are both planning to go away to college. Concerned about how she will cope when they have gone, she writes a story about the emotions a mother experiences when her last child leaves home and she finds herself alone

with her husband for the first time in over twenty years. The story, told from the heart, offers an identifiable situation for the readership of several women's magazines.

## CHECKLIST

1. Are your stories too long for the popular fiction market?
2. Are you writing purely for a specialist genre?
3. Do you enjoy reading women's magazine fiction?
4. Can you genuinely relate to the readership of the magazines you have selected?
5. Do you enjoy writing fictional stories?

## ASSIGNMENT

Select a magazine you enjoy and which considers unsolicited fiction and write down four themes you feel would appeal to the readership. Choose the one you feel most comfortable with and draft out a storyline, making sure that your characters fall into the right age group and reflect the right attitudes. Now write the story, keeping as close as possible to the length, style and format of your chosen story slot.

Are your stories too long for the popular fiction market?

# 7
# Caring for your Characters

## IDENTIFYING WITH YOUR CHARACTERS

### Being the man in a woman's world

It is a common misconception among male writers that by using a female pseudonym when re-submitting a previously rejected manuscript, an unsuitable story will magically become acceptable to women's magazine editors.

Nothing could be further from the truth. A surprising number of men write very successfully for the women's market and a masculine name is neither a help nor a hindrance to having work accepted for publication.

Whilst many male writers achieve most success with twist-end stories, there is also a healthy sprinkling producing fiction for lifestyle and romance slots. Contrary to common belief, it is not necessary to be female to relate either to the readership or to the problems that beset their daily lives.

For example, the following topics are equally relevant to both sexes and are ideal themes for magazine short stories:

● attending a much-needed job interview

● bringing up a child single-handed

● facing life after being widowed/divorced

● falling in love

● finding yourself deep in debt

● imminent parenthood

● supermarket shopping

● the pressures of unemployment on a relationship

● unfair treatment at work.

## Seeing life through the eyes of your characters

Characters in magazine fiction must:

● reflect the age and social status of your readership

● be people to whom your readers can relate

● do the same sort of jobs as your readers

● live in the same sort of areas and homes as your readers

● have the same dreams, hopes and fears as your readers

● use the same vocabulary as your readers.

A good short story is one which takes a little bit of daily life and gives the reader a smattering of hope. It allows the reader to believe that love can overcome any obstacle, that good does triumph over evil and that it is possible to win through against all the odds.

## Liking the people you portray

Liking your characters is perhaps the most important aspect of fiction writing. If you don't care whether or not they achieve their aims, then nor will the reader.

Even if the villain is nasty through and through, you have to care what happens to them. They must have a vulnerable spot to which the reader can relate. This should not excuse their actions but should give them a realistic reason for going off the rails.

## Sympathising with the heroine

Your heroine must be attractive without being too glamorous. She should look good enough for the readers to like her and sympathise with her plight but not so beautiful that she could never possibly be mistaken for one of them.

Her problems will be instantly recognisable to the readership as the following examples demonstrate:

● not wanting to be hurt by a partner again

● choosing between love and a career

● feeling under pressure to have a baby

● suspecting her partner is having an affair

● rebuilding a relationship after splitting up.

## Relating to the viewpoint character

The viewpoint character is the one whose story you are telling either in the:

● first person viewpoint, i.e. 'I never thought this would happen to me'.

or in the

● third person viewpoint, i.e. 'She never thought this would happen to her'.

The advantage of using first person viewpoint is that the writer can assume the role of the central character and so relate to them completely. With third person, you are removed from the protagonist and there is a danger that you will switch from one character to another, making the story confusing and losing all-reader identification.

However, whilst first person may appear to be the best option, it can be a very limiting style and some fiction editors prefer the more flexible third person viewpoint in the stories they publish.

## Avoiding viewpoint switches

One way to avoid switching viewpoint is to remember that the viewpoint character is the only one whose thoughts are known to you. For example:

Karen glanced nervously from one to the other. She knew she was right for the job but would they agree?

'Congratulations, Miss Carson,' at the warmth of his smile, Karen felt the tension flow from her body, 'We'll be happy to take you on,' he lifted an enquiring eyebrow, 'When will you be free to start work?'

Although the interviewer is speaking, we are seeing the scene entirely through Karen's thoughts and emotions, making her the viewpoint character.

## SIMPLIFYING THE PLOT

Because magazine fiction is designed to be a kind of 'quick fix' read, plots tend to be rather one-dimensional.

Every story must have conflict between the characters, in the form of differences of opinion between them or obstacles they have to overcome. In fiction, conflict does not necessarily mean that your characters are constantly fighting with one another. It is simply a device by which you introduce problems for your characters to solve, either between them or together as a couple.

## Changing the lives of your characters

In very short shorts, 500-1,500 words, the story is simply an incident in a character's life. However, no matter how small the incident, it should leave you in no doubt that the character's life will have been irrevocably changed. In a longer story, you may have room for perhaps one minor sub-plot but nothing too complicated or you will be unable to do it justice within the confines of a short story format.

## Keeping it simple

Take, for example, a storyline about a young, newly married couple moving into an old family house. The conflict could be that they bought the house with the idea of starting a family but having scraped together the purchase price, there is now no way they can afford to have a child.

This will provide your central theme, but to give it more substance, perhaps there is a history to the house. It's not a terribly grand property but they discover that it had belonged to one family for several generations. There is, your heroine feels, a wonderful homely atmosphere about the place. Looking up from the narrow hallway, she can visualise how it must have been, crammed full of happy, laughing children.

She decides to investigate the history of the original owners, offering a sub-plot in the form of the problems her predecessors encountered when setting up their home together. She discovers that they both began life in service but through hard work, managed to better themselves until they were in a position to marry and rent the old house. Not until their children had grown and were contributing to the family income, were they able to buy the house and achieve security for their old age.

The original theme about the newlyweds' dilemma will be kept to the forefront of the story but comparison with the past will enable the heroine to choose her course of action.

## Making the right choices

Her decision will be heavily influenced by the type of person she is and the readership of the magazine.

For a magazine aimed at independent career women, the sub-plot may serve as a warning to think about your motives before making the decision to have a baby. Looking at how tough life was for the children of impoverished parents in the past, the heroine may feel it is better to wait until she can afford to leave work and devote her time totally to her baby.

For a magazine that requires a more romantic outlook, the heroine will decide that it is not possible to put a price on happiness. She may not be able to give her child material things but judging by the previous occupants of her house, all you really need for your baby to thrive is love.

## SETTINGS AND BACKGROUNDS

For your readers to relate to the characters in your stories, the settings and backgrounds must be instantly recognisable.

Apart from an historical romance, it is unlikely that having your heroine living a privileged lifestyle in luxurious surroundings will cut much ice with the average women's magazine reader. Characters in magazine fiction tend to inhabit the following dwellings:

● council houses

● flats in high-rise blocks, converted houses or above shops

● 3-4 bedroomed semis

● bedsits.

Very occasionally, they live in old folks homes or thatched country cottages, but these are the exception rather than the rule.

Geographically, magazine fiction characters may live anywhere from John O'Groats to Lands End, in a rural community or on an inner-city housing estate. The only rule is that the reader must be able to identify with them.

## LISTENING IN ON CONVERSATIONS

Magazine stories contain a high proportion of dialogue and there are two main reasons for this:

1. Dialogue = Pace, i.e. keeps the story moving, and you must have a fast pace if you are to successfully fill the small slot allocated to you.

Listening in on conversations.

2. People love eavesdropping on other people's conversations.

## Describing the characters

One of the most effective methods of letting your readers know what is happening in a story is through the conversations your characters have with one another. Good dialogue should:

● describe the characters' appearance

● explain what has gone before

● give a hint of what is about to come

● move the story forward

● offer a clear insight into the characters' personalities.

We'll be looking at how you show the reader what is happening through a combination of dialogue and action in Chapter 9. It should be possible, however, to tell who is speaking to whom simply from the vocabulary used, without any description at all.

## Speaking naturally

Study the sentences below and see if you can tell who the characters are (answers on page 138). It should be quite clear not only who is speaking but also the person they are talking to:

1. 'Look, here's your mummy in this photo. You look just like her when she was your age.'

2. 'You won't regret this. I've been dying to have a go at your hair colour. I promise you won't recognise yourself. It'll take years off you.'

3. 'I'm pleased to tell you that the X-rays were clear. You've had a lucky escape this time but if you don't ease back on your workload and cut down on your smoking and drinking, you won't get away with it again.'

## Standing on the dialogue alone

For short passages, good dialogue will stand on its own without the need for any action or description at all. For example:

'Here, Linda, try this lipstick. I'd buy it like a shot if I had fair hair like you. The colour'll look great against your pale skin.
'D'you think so? I'm not sure. It looks a bit bright to me. I usually prefer reddish-browns to shocking pinks.'

It's quite obvious that the two characters are women friends out shopping and from their conversation, we know a little about them. We know that:

● Linda has fair hair and pale skin

● from her choice of lipstick, she's quite conservative in her appearance

● that her friend is much more lively and adventurous

● that her friend has a darker complexion and hair.

We also know which one is speaking and exactly what they are doing. Any description or action would be superfluous.

We can, however, change the characterisation by making a few alterations to the dialogue, still without using any description:

'Excuse me Madam, would you like to try this lipstick? I must say, I wouldn't hesitate to buy it if I had fair hair like you. The colour will set off your pale complexion beautifully.
'D'you think so? It looks a bit bright to me. I usually prefer reddish-browns to shocking pinks. Still, I suppose it's worth giving it a go.'

The conversation is intrinsically the same but by adding a few words and changing others, we have two entirely new characters, in the form of a sales girl on a cosmetic counter and an easy-going customer.

## SOLVING PROBLEMS

As mentioned above, conflict is vital to any work of fiction. In every story that you write, you must give your central character a problem to solve.

### Empowering your characters

Having created characters you care about, it can be tempting to try and sort out all their problems for them. An understandable emotion, but one which must be firmly squashed if you are to write effectively for the magazine market.

Many of your readers will identify with the problems in your stories and, although they won't expect solutions to be handed to them on a plate, will be looking for a note of hope in the stories you write.

The following solutions are just a few you should avoid at all costs:

● Timely intervention by a well-meaning elderly person, i.e. the wise old lady or gentleman who helps your character see the error of their ways.

- A useful coincidence, i.e. the guy chatting up your heroine reveals he is a plumber, car mechanic, plasterer or whatever who can fix her leak, engine or hole in her wall.

- A lottery win just in time to save the character from financial ruin.

- The boyfriend conveniently deciding to move out just as your heroine was going to break off their relationship.

## Working it out for themselves

Waving a metaphorical magic wand over the situation to waft all the problems away is a hopeless cheat. The reader wants to see how the characters cope and move on with their lives, so let them work it out for themselves. Put yourself in their place. What would you do if:

- Your car broke down?

- Your central heating packed up?

- You felt the need to confront your partner about your relationship?

OK, maybe in real life you would call the AA, pick a plumber at random from *Yellow Pages*, or squash any nagging doubts and just get on with your life, but that's not the stuff good fiction is made of.

You need to have your characters interacting with one another, so go back and think what your central character would do.

## Setting up the situation

Is she the capable type who can strip a car down and reassemble it without having six washers and a length of rubber hose leftover? If so, when her car breaks down, she'll fix it herself. To make a story out of that situation, you'll either have to set her somewhere isolated and scary or have her falling for a 'new' man who'll cook, clean and be prepared to be a stay-at-home dad when the first baby arrives.

## Seeking a manly shoulder

Today's heroines are unlikely to admit to actively seeking a man who will whisk them off to a life of domestic bliss. They may reluctantly be forced to confess to needing a man to perform traditionally masculine tasks but this will add to the conflict between them. On the whole, your female characters should be relatively self-sufficient.

## Switching roles

Male characters can be anything from caring single parents to male chauvinist pigs. They can be very sensitive and understanding about the problems their girlfriends and wives face. Alternatively, they could be total slobs, depending on the tone and style of the story and the magazine at which it is aimed.

Heroes can be just as concerned about developments in their relationships as their female counterparts and may be facing up to the problems associated with competition in the workplace, retirement, widowhood and getting on with the neighbours in just the same way.

## RAISING HOPES

Writers should aim for uplifting endings for their stories which may not necessarily be happy but will give the reader hope.

For example, a story aimed at a magazine for over-forties might have a widow new to the area as its central character. She and her husband retired to their dream bungalow but shortly after they arrived he died, leaving her alone in a strange town.

This situation is all too common and sadly one to which many older readers will relate. If the widow is portrayed as being unable to cope, it would be far too painful for many readers to handle. As a writer, you have a responsibility to your readers to find a way for her to come to terms with what has happened and move on with her life.

### Offering a way through

There are no instant solutions to this problem and your readers are well aware of that. There may, however, be a way through for them by offering them some options. Your central character could:

● sell up and move back to her old neighbourhood

● embark on a fund-raising project in memory of her husband

● take the first step to rebuilding a social life by inviting a neighbour to lunch

● volunteer to help with a planned community event

● book a trip to somewhere she has always wanted to go.

If the route you choose for your character offers just one reader a choice they hadn't previously considered, then it will be a huge achievement in your fiction-writing career.

## CASE STUDIES

### George tries his hand at murder

George is a crime fiction devotee in his late forties. He has successfully written some stories for a small press crime magazine he subscribes to and decides to try his hand at his wife's weekly women's magazine. The story, which he submits under the pen name, Georgina Flintlock, is about a henpecked wimp who is killed by his wife because he forgets to take her a cup of tea in bed before he leaves for work in the morning. The lack of realistic motive for murder combined with George's concern about revealing his true identity to his intended readership ensures a swift rejection.

## Rob switches roles

Rob is a computer programmer in his late twenties. His story, aimed at a women's magazine for the under-forties' market, has the reader following the protagonist through every stage of advanced pregnancy from food cravings, relaxation and breathing exercises, misgivings about the decision to have a baby and labour pains to the emotional high of giving birth, until the twist end reveals that the central 'I' character is, in fact, the baby's father. The story is accepted and published under Rob's own name.

## CHECKLIST

1.  Do you care what happens to your characters?

2.  Will magazine readers relate to the characters and situations in your story?

3.  Will your story fit into a specific magazine 'slot'?

4.  Is the dialogue in your story realistic?

5.  Will your readership relate to the vocabulary you use?

## ASSIGNMENT

Magazine short stories reflect everyday situations. Write a confrontational conversation between a couple under stress packing to go on holiday. As the dialogue between them develops, see if you can expand the scene into a short story.

# 8
# Finding the Right Format

## ROMANCING THE READER

As mentioned in previous chapters, the market for romantic fiction has shrunk over the past few years.

### Waiting for Mr Right

Whilst characters in magazine fiction still fall in love and even get married, the whole concept of 'waiting for Mr Right' to come along and sweep the heroine off her feet is no longer an acceptable theme.

Today's romantic fiction is all about making choices. The central character will have to decide her course of action from a number of options:

- Does she commit herself to marriage or retain her independence by staying single?

- Does she give up her career to follow her man or must he give up his to follow her?

- Is a good sex life the basis on which to commit herself to a long-term relationship?

- Is she prepared to work on a relationship with the children of the man she loves?

- Having divorced her husband, should she now give him another chance?

- Can she risk falling in love again after being badly hurt before?

### Laughing at love

All the themes listed above overlap between the categories of romance and lifestyle.

However, there is still room for some old-fashioned romance, where the girl is out to trap her man, but these usually have more than a hint of humour about them. They tend to be either:

● quirky tales where the central character appears to be disinterested in her quarry but tricks him into asking her out

or

● typically triangular tales, where the heroine is involved with one rather unsavoury character, whilst another much more acceptable but less exciting prospect waits patiently in the wings.

With the second type of story, the humour generally comes in the form of romantic banter between the hopeful lover and the heroine. Comparing it with the serious, often demanding relationship she has with her boyfriend, realisation slowly dawns on the central character that the couple that laughs together, stays together.

## Making love

Love scenes can be quite explicit in some magazines. Some of the titles aimed at the under-forties are prepared to include stories with an erotic flavour, although as with all romantic fiction, the emphasis should always be on love, rather than sex.

For *Bella's* 2,000-word romances, fiction editor Linda O'Byrne's guidelines state that the story should have:

A central love interest, plenty of conflict, warmth, emotion and an understanding that physical sex exists between people in love! There should be a happy or hopeful ending. Not usually a traditional boy-meets-girl story but rather the problems encountered in an established relationship. The main characters should both play a part in resolving their difficulties.

## LOOKING AT LIFESTYLES

For many of today's magazines, the emphasis for their short story characters is on lifestyle rather than romance.

## Living the lives of your readers

These stories reflect the lives of the readership and like their romantic counterparts, offer choices, rather than solutions. Lifestyle topics include:

● examining attitudes to in-laws

● handling sensitive situations in the workplace

● becoming an 'empty-nester', i.e. seeing your children grow up and leave home

● inviting ex-spouses and their partners to weddings

- adopted children tracking down their natural parents
- meeting the child you gave up for adoption
- setting up home with a step-family
- rebuilding your life after a tragedy.

In other words, anything at all that your readership might experience in their own lives. Providing it is handled sensitively, almost any topic can be covered, but every story must end on a note of hope.

## TWISTING THE TALE

Twist or surprise-end stories feature in the vast majority of popular women's weeklies.

### Deceiving the reader

There are two main types of twist stories:

1. Those in which the central character appears to be getting away with something but is effectively hoist with his or her own petard at the end.

2. Those in which the characters are not who or what they appear to be.

The twist author sets out to deceive the reader and achieves this by a combination of strong characterisation, subtle double-edged clues and a somewhat quirky attitude of mind.

### Setting up the signposts

One of the commonest misconceptions about twist-end stories is that the key is in concealing the truth from the reader. In fact, in order to achieve the desired result, it is essential that you keep the reader fully informed by sprinkling subtle 'signposts' or clues throughout the story.

For example, in the following extract from a story entitled 'Act Your Age!' who do you think the characters are?

> Mandy eyed her mother's back impatiently, 'For heavens' sake,' she muttered, dropping her bag noisily on the kitchen floor. 'Mum! Hurry up! I'll be late for school at this rate.'

Hopefully, you have correctly identified them as mother and daughter, but what about Mandy's age? If you've assumed she is a teenager, then that is just the result I was aiming for.

However, things are never what they seem in a twist story, so it helps to consider possible alternatives. As the story progresses, it becomes clear that Mandy is becoming increasingly unhappy about her divorced mother's relationship with their recently widowed next door neighbour:

'Mum, you're not going out tonight are you?' she frowned at the large gold earrings slapping at her mother's jaw, wishing she could turn the clock back to the days when it was just the two of them and she behaved and dressed like a real mum.

Mandy had even teased her once that, with her neat perm and her frilly apron, she looked exactly like the mother in those old first reading books – where the children played ball with the dog and father wore sleeveless pullovers.

Adèle Ramet, *Bella Summer Special* 1997

By now you should be getting a bit suspicious because, if you think about it, mothers haven't dressed this way for around forty years.

In fact, by the end of the story, it is revealed that far from being a teenager, Mandy is a school teacher, well into her thirties. Whilst her mother is, perhaps, a little long in the tooth for her new T-shirt and jeans image, having devoted her life to single-handedly raising a daughter, she has every intention of grabbing what she perceives to be her last chance of happiness.

## Cheating never works

At no time was the reader ever cheated in this story. Although the initial impression is of a sulky teenager, it is the phrase, 'late for school,' that immediately plants the misleading image in the reader's mind. However, the phrase could just as easily be uttered by a teacher as a pupil.

As with all other forms of magazine fiction, situations and settings must be instantly recognisable and the twist writer capitalises on this by gently nudging the reader towards forming the wrong conclusion.

For more detailed information on the construction of twist-end stories and market opportunities for them, see my book in the How To Books Successful Writing series entitled *Creating a Twist in the Tale.*

## EXPLORING THE UNKNOWN

There is a growing trend to look to the paranormal for inspiration. Magazines like *Bella, Best* and *Woman's Weekly* will all consider stories with a ghostly theme.

The majority of these stories tend to be featured in the twist slots, although romantic stories can also have a spiritual dimension.

**Empathising with an entity**

Ghostly characters are amazingly similar to their flesh and blood counterparts. They, too, have backgrounds, failing relationships and problems to solve. They may also perform any one of the following functions:

● helping the central character make the right choice

● strengthening the central character's resolve

● supporting them through a difficult time

● giving them an insight into their future

● offering comfort and hope

● providing the humour in a story.

Even a mischievous spirit can be instrumental in solving a problem,
albeit unintentionally.

**Dabbling in the occult**

As a general rule, it is unwise to dabble in the occult, but there is one
exception to this rule and that is Halloween.

Seasonal stories are always welcome and providing they are a force
for good, witches can and do make a regular appearance at this time of
year. However, few self-respecting modern witches would be seen dead
in the traditional black cloak and pointed hat.

Today's witches are usually indistinguishable in appearance and
lifestyle from any other characters and in common with them, they have
updated their image and their attitudes.

The only two ingredients which have tended to remain unchanged are
the black cat and the broomstick. Fiction editors know that, as far as
their readers are concerned, cutting all their links with traditional values
never really pays.

## FACING FUTURISTIC IDEAS

At the present time, there is only one women's weekly prepared to even
consider manuscripts with a science fiction theme and that is *Bella* magazine.

Until recently, their twist-in-the-tale would, very occasionally, have a
futuristic theme. In the main, these centred around test-tube reproduction, defrosting frozen males for the use by all-female societies, and life
in an environmentally damaged eco-system.

## Chilling out

However, 1997 saw the introduction of two-part 'chillers' in similar vein to the television series *The X Files*. At 1,800 words per episode, this innovative concept for women's weekly magazine fiction is the closest to a serial that *Bella* is prepared to go at the present time. Although other magazines have attempted to introduce so-called 'chilling' tales, this is the first to deal specifically with the issues of government secrecy, alien beings and futuristic forces on our way of life.

Whether or not the stories are set in the future, however, the format remains the same. The characters' emotions and reactions must be instantly recognisable to the readership, who must be able to relate to the attitudes and behaviour portrayed.

## GOING BACK IN TIME

The market for historical stories is another area that is shrinking rapidly. Perhaps the best opportunities in this field are to be found in magazines specialising in romantic fiction.

## Picturing the scene

In order to write effective historical fiction, both you and the reader must be able to picture the scene you are setting. The following points are essential:

● in-depth knowledge of the period in which your story is set

● vocabulary which reflects the manner of speech of the period

● accuracy with regard to costumes and hairstyles

● a knowledge of the modes of transport and journey times

● accurate knowledge of the food consumed and how it would be prepared

● in-depth understanding of the etiquette of the period.

## DEVISING SERIALS

Because of the detail required in order to effectively convey an historical background, these tend to be featured as serials, rather than one-off short stories.

Markets for serials are very limited, but one major title still prepared to take them is *Women's Weekly*. Fiction editor Gaynor Davies offers the following tips for new writers in her helpful and comprehensive writers' guidelines:

Serials should have all the compelling qualities of short stories – strong characterisation and background – and must also have riveting cliffhangers to keep the reader going back to the newsagent week after week! There should be a central 'hook' to hang the action on; an emotional or practical dilemma which the heroine has to face. A strong subplot and well-researched background are essential. Historicals are just as welcome as contemporary serials.

Serials can be between two and five parts. The opening instalment is 6,800 words and each subsequent instalment is 3,800 words.

You may submit the whole of your manuscript, or just the first part with a brief synopsis. A synopsis alone cannot be considered; we need to be able to assess your style too.

## CASE STUDIES

### Penny looks back

Before her youngest child started school, Penny was too busy to read the historical novels she loves and her reading was confined to a weekly women's magazine. Convinced that she can write better fiction than the short twist stories currently being published, she writes a torrid Regency romance. The rejection slip bears a curt note urging Penny to read the magazine to establish content and style.

### Jane foresees the future

Jane is a grandmother in her fifties. Her grandson's preoccupation with computers sparks off an idea for a story centred around high-tech communication with the spirit world. Whilst the ghost comes from a previous century, Jane's futuristic outlook brings the story bang up-to-date for the modern magazine market.

## CHECKLIST

1. Are the themes of your stories relevant to today's magazine readers?

2. Could your story be expanded to serial length?

3. Is any historical content accurate?

4. Does your story have a genuine twist?

5. Are you aiming your story at the right market?

## ASSIGNMENT

Read the following passage then answer the questions to help you decide whether the story should be a romance, lifestyle or twist-in-the-tale:

A married couple have just moved into the neighbourhood. It is Saturday morning and the husband has stayed at home to look after their six-month-old baby whilst the wife has gone shopping. She returns with a friend, a girl she was at school with, who, it turns out, lives just round the corner. The minute he sets eyes on the friend, the husband's jaw drops and he goes quite pale.*

* *Note*: If you prefer, you can turn the situation round, so that the husband brings a male friend home and it is the wife who reacts.

1. How old are the characters?

2. What are their names?

3. What do they look like?

4. Do they have jobs and if so, what do they do?

5. What is the cause of the spouse's reaction?

6. How will they deal with the situation?

7. Which character do you relate to most strongly?

8. What happens next?

Are you aiming your story at the right market?

# 9
# Fitting a Specific Slot

## BEGINNING WITH THE ENDING

Wherever there is a fiction slot in a magazine, the requirements are specific. Every short story submitted for publication must be:

- written to the specified length
- in the magazine's house style
- in the required format, i.e. romance, twist, lifestyle, etc.

Each story must also have:

- a Beginning
- a Middle
- an End.

Telling the tale in a set number of words gives you very little leeway for extra characters, sub-plots or extravagant vocabulary.

Neither can you afford to let your story run on until it comes to what you consider to be its natural conclusion. If you are unsure how long your manuscript should be, take the latest issue of your chosen publication, find the short story and physically count the words on the printed page.

### Working towards a goal

In order to be sure of fitting your story into the required word length, before you begin to write it, you must know how it is going to end.

In the same way that the opening to an article reveals immediately what it is about, the beginning of a short story must 'hook' the reader's interest. You must then use the middle to hold that interest, delivering everything you promised in the first paragraphs.

Finally, the ending serves to tie everything up in a satisfactory manner. Without a clear goal in mind, however, you could well wander away from the point.

In fact, a short story is constructed in exactly the same manner as a non-fiction article. In the absence of an outline, you can easily lose sight of your storyline and by the time you come to wind it up, you won't be sure who is doing what to whom, why they are doing it or what the result will be.

## Twisting the tale

In a straightforward romance or lifestyle story, there is some room for flexibility with the ending, although straying too far from the original plan could cause problems.

In a twist story, however, knowing the ending is imperative. The entire construction of a twist story is based on leading the reader initially away from the ending and then veering back round towards it for the closing line.

Unless you know the last line before you start, it is impossible to plant the misleading signposts you need to achieve an effective twist in the tale.

## Opening the story

The opening to your story must:

● introduce the characters

● set the scene

● grab the reader's attention

● hook them into reading more by giving a hint of what is to come.

Take a look at the two following openings and see which you think has the most impact:

*Opening A*
The morning dawned warm and sunny, offering the promise of another glorious day. Davinda wandered lazily over to the window and gave a little sigh of happiness. What a lovely home she and Miles had together, she thought, leaning out to wave at him as he mowed the immaculate lawn.

*Opening B*
Shielding her eyes from the sun's glare, Denise leaned out of the window, 'Mike! Hey, Mike, come quick, I need you!' Irritably, she realised he couldn't hear her above the racket made by his precious lawnmower.

## Making an instant impression

In Opening A, the action is so slow as to be non-existent. As far as the reader can tell, the state of the weather has little relevance to the plot and Davinda is somewhat smug and self-satisfied.

There is no hint that anything is amiss, as she and Miles are apparently living an idyllic life together. So unless she suddenly falls out of the window she is waving from, there is no reason to continue reading the story.

## Introducing conflict

Opening B is quite different. The sunshine, so attractively portrayed in the first example, is now an irritant in Denise's eyes.

The characters' names have been changed to ones with which the readership will relate and something is definitely wrong between them. When Denise calls to Mike and he fails to respond, she refers to his 'precious' lawnmower. It is, both metaphorically and physically, forming a barrier between them and in order to find out more, the reader is compelled to continue.

## Pulling the reader on

The middle of the story should contain all the information required to hold the reader's interest. This includes:

● background information

● conflict between the characters

● a clear insight into their personalities

● plenty of dialogue between the characters

● the gradual unfolding of the storyline.

## Reaching the required ending

Before you can give your full attention to all the above points, you must have an ending in mind.

To see how this works, we need to return to Denise and Mike and decide how we want to resolve their conflict. Let's assume it's a romance/lifestyle story. First, we need to establish who they are and the biggest hint to this is their names.

This is one of the quickest methods of establishing characterisation as a simple test will reveal. Look at the names listed in Figure 7 and write down the age and social status they suggest to you.

Denise and Mike fall believably into the 30–50 age range and it is clear that they have a comfortable lifestyle which, in this context, gives another clue to their age.

Give the age and social status suggested by the names listed below.

| Name | Age | Social status |
| --- | --- | --- |
| Bert | | |
| Dean | | |
| Denise | | |
| Jarvis | | |
| Kylie | | |
| Lavinia | | |
| Lil | | |
| Mark | | |

Fig. 7. Characterisation test.

You can alter this impression by moving things around, putting them in a different setting, shortening or lengthening their names when they speak to one another.

## Ending happily ever after

Bearing in mind that the opening must give a hint of what is to come, it is obvious that Mike's preoccupation with the lawn is a bone of contention between him and Denise.

She needs him but can't get a response from him and this could be seen as a metaphor for their marriage. If the story is to end happily, we have to get them to face up to the problems they are experiencing and work them out together.

Now we have a basis on which to form the middle of our story. We need now to think about the following points:

● the background – the cause of the problems

● the conflict – what is going to bring the situation to a head

● the solution– how they will achieve the desired happy ending in under 2,000 words.

### Giving the reader a 'quick fix'

As we saw in the previous chapter, the length of these stories confines the writer to offering quick-fix solutions. For Denise and Mike, we need a trigger to make them rethink their relationship.

Perhaps Denise is calling Mike because she has received a letter from their son, Kevin, asking her to come and house-sit for him whilst he goes away for a month's backpacking with his friends. Having a grown-up son living away from home confirms the age of the characters and offers an insight into how they relate to one another.

Mike's attitude to the news of his wife's impending departure comes in the form of a resigned shrug of assent, implying that this isn't the first time he's been dumped in favour of his selfish son. As Denise prattles on about the food she's packed in the freezer for him and the arrangements she's made for her absence, it becomes even clearer that for years, whenever her son has called, she's always come running.

More insight is provided by comparison between the two men. The son is active, earns good money, does exciting things. Poor old Mike is a dull, boring plodder by comparison.

However, Denise appears to have forgotten something absolutely vital about her husband. She doesn't seem to consider that without his hard work and devotion to his family, things might have been very different both for her and the son she idolises.

### Attaining a satisfactory resolution
In a story of this type, we need a resolution that will be satisfactory to the reader, one which opens Denise's eyes to the fact that she has been neglecting her husband in favour of her son.

Having begun with Mike in the garden, we can structure the story so that it ends with him going dejectedly back to his beloved lawn in a way that makes Denise understand where her priorities lie.

Watching the lonely figure in the garden, she suddenly realises whom she has to thank for the fact that their son is an outgoing and independent young man. She finally accepts that it's time to leave Kevin to get on with his own life. Her place is at her husband's side, sharing the home they have made together.

## USING THE RIGHT VOCABULARY

For many novice authors, the art of writing involves using as many long words as possible in order to impress the reader.

### Keeping it simple
In fact, a good rule for any writer to follow is that if you think your reader will have to stop and look up one of your words in a dictionary, cut the word and rewrite the sentence.

The principle of using vocabulary that your reader will understand and relate to is not simply a modern device favoured by the women's magazine market. The poet Horace, who died in 8 BC, stated that:

You will have written exceptionally well if, by skillful arrangement of your words, you have made an ordinary one seem original.

The fact that his works have endured to the present day bears this out, so take a tip from Horace and use vocabulary which is realistic and easy for your reader to understand.

## Speeding and slowing the pace

The following examples demonstrate how you can speed and slow the pace with vocabulary:

● Nestling drowsily back against the softness of the cushions, the gentle melody lulled her dreamily into a deep, peaceful slumber. (20 words)

● Thumping the cushions into submission, she burrowed her head into them in a vain attempt to shut out the shrill music penetrating every fibre of her being. (28 words)

Despite the fact that the second example is longer by eight words, the effect of the vocabulary is actually faster and sharper than the first.

By using soft words like 'drowsily', 'softness', 'gentle', 'lulled', 'dreamily' and 'peaceful', the atmosphere created is one of relaxation and calm.

In the second example, hard words such as, 'thumping', 'submission', 'burrowed', 'shrill' and 'penetrating' not only give a much sharper edge to the sentence but also a feeling of action and movement.

## Using short, sharp sentences

Another way of increasing the pace is to keep the sentences short and sharp. Short sentences are easy to read and keep the action moving.

In stories of between 500 and 1,200 words, short sentences are vital if you are to get the point over before you reach the end. For longer romances, you have a little leeway to lengthen the sentences and to give your story a gentler, slower feel.

However, you will still be working to a maximum target of around 5,000 words and even with the 6,800-word opening episode of a serial for *Woman's Weekly*, you have to build up the pace to a cliffhanging climax to ensure the reader is compelled to read next week's instalment.

## SHOWING THROUGH ACTION AND DIALOGUE

One piece of advice commonly given by all writing tutors is to 'show' not 'tell'.

## Showing not telling

This is the means by which you show what is going on through a combination of action and dialogue rather than simply narrating a tale.

To this end, when writing dialogue, the first words that should be discarded are 'he/she said'. These are possibly the most superfluous words in any short story and along with others in similar vein, should be avoided for the following reasons:

● They slow the pace.

● They increase the total wordcount.

● They are a clumsy method of writing dialogue.

For example, compare sentences 1 and 2.

1.  'I don't know how you can say that,' <u>he said as he continued to pack his suitcase</u>, 'You know I've never so much as looked at another woman.'

2.  "I don't know how you can say that,' <u>he patted the last shirt neatly into place in his suitcase</u>, 'You know I've never so much as looked at another woman.'

The first example tells us very little about that man, except that he has been accused of playing around and that he is packing a suitcase.

In the second, we know a little more about him. We know that he packs neatly and that he appears unconcerned about any accusations of infidelity made against him.

## Altering the tone

We can, however, alter the tone by changing his reaction:

3.  'I don't know how you can say that,' <u>he flung his clothes angrily into the suitcase</u>, 'you know I've never so much as looked at another woman.'

In the third example, he indicates through his actions how annoyed he is, but in neither example 2 nor 3 are the words 'he said' necessary.

In both, the scene is conveyed or 'shown' through a combination of dialogue and action.

## Finding alternative words

Of course, it is possible to find alternatives to the word 'said'. Any one of the following would sum up the mood of a character:

● bellowed

- exclaimed

- growled

- grunted

- murmured

- muttered

- roared

- screamed

- screeched

- shouted

- whispered

- yelled.

No doubt you could double the number of verbs on this list with ease, but the effect of replacing 'said' with an alternative is negligible. There will be occasions when, for practical and/or stylistic purposes, the use of 'he/she said' or its equivalent is essential. For the most part, however, it is probably best to cross the whole list through and consign it to the wastebin.

## KEEPING IT SHORT WITH FLASHBACK

By now, you will understand the importance of producing manuscripts which fit their allotted space within the pages of your chosen magazine.

### Filling in the background

However, if a story is to have any substance, we have to find a way to fill in the relevant background information to the storyline without pushing up the wordcount.

The most effective method of doing this is through flashback, i.e. flashing back into the past and then returning the reader rapidly to the present. Flashback performs the following functions:

- It describes the characters.

- It tells the reader what has gone before.

- It fills in the gaps in the storyline.

- It gives a hint of what is to come.

Returning to Denise and Mike's story, it is important that the reader knows how their marriage came to be under threat. Flashback is ideal for this as the following passage demonstrates.

'I've had a letter from Kevin,' Denise searched her husband's face for signs of resistance, 'He wants me to go and house-sit for him.'

'**Again?**' Mike lifted his baseball cap to scratch the thinning hair beneath it, 'How long for **this time?**'

'Oh, only a month or two,' Denise deliberately kept her tone light, '**I knew you wouldn't mind** and it is so nice for him just to be able to take off when he feels like it without worrying about things at home.'

'I wouldn't know,' slowly replacing his cap, Mike turned towards the French windows, '**We haven't had a chance to get away for ages,** you're that busy running after your beloved son.'

'He's your son too,' Denise chewed her bottom lip, **determined not to let this flare up into yet another row,** 'You should be proud that he's done so well for himself. He's not a stick-in-the-mud like, well,' she hesitated, 'like some men I could . . .'

'Like his father you mean,' dejectedly, Mike made his way out to the patio, 'I'll get on with the lawn,' he glanced back over his shoulder, 'Let me known when you're leaving and **don't worry about stocking the freezer this time,** I can cook my own meals you know. I'm not entirely helpless.' (212 words)

This entire passage only amounts to just over 200 words but the flashbacks, shown in bold, give a great deal of information to the reader.

They are only tiny snippets or 'flashes' but they give a clear idea of what has gone before, that everything is about to be repeated and that if nothing is done to prevent it, something is going to crack.

## KNOWING WHAT TO CUT AND WHAT TO KEEP

As we have seen, flashback is an essential aid to feeding in the background whilst keeping the wordcount down.

### Cutting and tightening

One of the most important disciplines a writer has to master if they wish to write fiction for the magazine market is economy with words. Bear in mind that almost everything you write will be improved by cutting and you can cut almost everything you write.

However, cutting your manuscript to a specified word length is not simply a matter of taking out the odd superfluous word or phrase. It also involves tightening the piece, turning sentences and phrases around, finding a more appropriate word, in order to produce a highly polished manuscript.

Knowing what to cut and what to keep.

### Picking out the important points

The following passage is 55 words long. Read it through, then cut it to at least half this length without losing the basic information.

> When she got out of the bus, she found that her skirt was covered in deep creases and she had to bend down to grab hold of the hem and pull it hard to try and straighten the material so that it looked nice and smart as it had when she had begun her journey.

A suggested rewrite is on page 138.

You could simply turn the piece round a little, cutting out all the superfluous words in the process. Alternatively you could alter the piece by adding dialogue, to 'show' what is happening, rather than narrating it, as is the case at the moment.

Whichever method you select, one thing is certain, an editor expects a story submitted for a 2,000-word slot to be roughly around that length. As with articles, it is permissible to be within 100 words either way but any more than this is pushing your luck.

### Losing the best bits

Ideally, it is better if your story is too long than too short as this should mean that it has plenty of substance to it.

Your first action should be to seek out the best, most eloquently poetic phrase in the whole piece and no matter how tough on your creative bent it may be, lose it. Take comfort in the fact that if you don't cut it, the editor almost certainly will as the more flowery the phraseology, the more likely it is to provide an unwelcome and distracting piece of self-indulgence on the part of the writer.

## Expanding the story

Packing everything you need for an effective story in around 1,000 words is extremely difficult, so when a story comes up too short, it is a sign that something vital has been omitted.

Go through it carefully and check that there is sufficient substance to the storyline. If you are sure that there is, then perhaps the background is too sketchy, or the dialogue is weak.

Never, ever 'pad' out a story by sliding in an extra character or situation to bring the piece up to length. A good short story is carefully planned from beginning to end and it is pointless trying to patch in extra pieces to stretch it into shape.

## CASE STUDIES

### Rachel needs an ending

Rachel is in her forties, the mother of three children. As soon as she has an idea for a story, she sits down to write it without any idea how it will end. As a result, she finds herself wandering away from the main theme and although she is very creative, she has never yet managed to finish any of the stories she has begun to write.

### Darren listens to his customers

Darren is in his mid-twenties, a soft furnishings salesman in a department store. He attends a creative writing evening class and acting on his tutor's advice to listen to how his customers relate to one another as they try out different armchairs, beds and sofas, his dialogue writing skills have improved by leaps and bounds. He is developing a real talent for writing well-constructed twist-in-the-tale stories, showing what is happening through a combination of realistic dialogue and action.

## CHECKLIST

1.   Do you know how your story is going to end before you begin?

2.   Is your story the right length for the slot you are aiming at?

3.    Is your vocabulary clear and easy to understand?

4.    Have you 'shown' the reader what is happening through a combination of dialogue and action?

5.    Does your story have a satisfactory resolution?

## ASSIGNMENT

If your story comes up too short, read it through to ensure that you have sufficient:

● background information

● description of the setting and characters

● interaction between the characters

● substance to the story.

Is your story the right length for the slot you are aiming at?

# 10
# Working as a Freelance

## ESTABLISHING A REPUTATION

There is a school of thought in the cynical world of the freelance article writer which states that, regardless of quality, all an editor really wants from you is manuscripts that are:

1. easy to read

2. on their desk by the deadline

3. written to the required length.

### Providing the quality

The above rules are important ones which are disregarded at your peril, but quality is more important than some cynics may believe. In order to meet the three requirements, you must be at a certain level of competence to start with. Clarity both in your writing and in the appearance of your manuscript is essential.

### Meeting deadlines

It is inconceivable that anyone serious about writing topical articles should not meet their editorial deadlines, but it has been known.

Thanks to faxes and E-Mail, many of the problems associated with postal delays have been eliminated, but the lack of just one piece of vital information or worse still, your computer crashing at the crucial moment, could be disastrous.

Should you be faced with an unavoidable delay, bite the bullet and contact the editor immediately, preferably with a contingency plan close at hand.

### Writing to length

Writing to length can be a difficult skill to master. If an editor is to employ you on a regular basis, you have to convince them that they can rely on you to produce work as close as possible to their exact specifications.

We'll be looking at marketing and presentation of manuscripts in Chapter 11, but for now, let's assume that the editor has accepted your first piece. Whether or not the manuscript is a fictional story or a factual article makes no difference. For it to be publishable, it will be the right length, format and style for the magazine.

However, the editor may feel that some alterations are necessary before the piece can be used. Should this be the case, don't quibble, just do it. Follow the editor's suggestions and re-submit the piece as quickly as possible.

Alternatively, the editor may change the piece without referring to you. Avoid the temptation to complain about it. Study the alterations and tailor your next manuscript accordingly.

### Meeting the editor's brief

In addition to being sure your manuscripts will always meet any agreed deadlines, an editor needs to know that:

● it is possible to discuss alterations with you

● you will do your best to rewrite along the lines you discussed

● you will accept any decision not to go ahead with publication of uncommissioned material

● if you are asked to produce something, you will do your best to comply.

### DELIVERING THE GOODS

In addition to the usual seasonal highs and lows, magazine and newspaper editors can suddenly find themselves with an empty slot and nothing to fill it.

### Keeping a stock of fillers

Fiction editors complain bitterly that, despite having stacks of unsuitable unsolicited stories cluttering their offices, the number of publishable manuscripts in stock at any one time is frightenly small.

Not having a suitable article available to coincide with an event of national or international importance is a feature editor's nightmare. Whether a national, regional or local publication, editors need a regular supply of material which reflect items of current topical interest.

### Giving them what they want

The situation you want to aim for is one where, when an editor gets an idea for a new feature, your name pops into their head.

Having phoned and asked you to produce something, preferably yesterday, preferably with photographs and probably 'on spec', the editor is not going to expect a refusal. Should that be your response, it is unlikely that you'll be asked to provide anything again for that publication, unless you have a cast-iron reason for your irrational behaviour.

Once you've agreed to write the piece, no matter how difficult you find it, somehow or other you must deliver the goods. The completed manuscript must, of course, be:

1. easy to read

2. on the editor's desk by the deadline

3. written to the required length.

## COMING UP WITH A BETTER IDEA

Occasionally, an editor will suggest an idea for a feature that simply doesn't hang together.

Perhaps you recently tried something similar and discovered that there was insufficient mileage in it for a satisfactory article. Under these circumstances, rather than attempting to tell an editor that their idea won't work, it will be much more productive to come up with an alternative.

### Talking it through

Once you have proved that you can produce work of a consistently high standard on a regular basis, then you should be able to persuade your editor to listen to any suggestions you may have.

At the end of the day, you may have to produce two features, one based on your idea and one on theirs, but that will be a small price to pay and if they both work out, could lead to you writing a whole series.

## ATTENDING PRESS FUNCTIONS

Invitations to press functions are included in every editor and columnist's mail. As a specialist feature writer, once your name is known, you too, will be invited to attend the launch of a new product, book, television series or film.

If you've never been to one before, it can initially be quite exciting to have the chance to rub shoulders with the rich and famous or be one of the first people to try out a new product, but after a while, this does begin to pall.

Experienced freelances gradually become more selective about the events they attend, aware that they could be on the receiving end of any of the following:

● a slap-up meal at a luxury venue

● an opportunity to interview a well-known personality

● a large goodie bag of free samples.

However, at some of these events, you may be lucky to get a glass of lukewarm wine in a plastic cup and a hastily put-together press pack.

## Making contacts

Travel to and from press functions can prove expensive, so you want to be sure it is worth your while. Not all the invitations you receive will be from unfamiliar sources. Many emanate from contacts you have made in your own area of expertise. If, for example, you write a regular gardening column, you will almost certainly be invited to attend the press day of at least one national flower show.

As you visit each stand, you will meet public relations and marketing representatives keen for you to feature their products in your column. Your name will be added to their mailing list and more invitations will begin to arrive.

## Getting something for nothing

As a representative of the press, you will be entitled to free entry to most trade shows, but nobody gives you anything for nothing. You may be fortunate enough to receive the odd free sample or heavily discounted new product. You may be entertained royally at each contact's stand, but your welcoming hosts will want something in return.

Just as your editors will expect the articles you send them to be up to scratch, so the trade contacts you make will expect to see their products featured in the publications that you represent. You should be able to guarantee that the article you intend to write will appear in at least one reputable publication in time to coincide with any planned publicity drives.

If you can offer even wider coverage, so much the better and as you will soon discover, the hospitality offered to you will increase and, sadly, decrease in direct relation to:

● the number of reputable magazines which publish your work

● the circulation figures of the publications in which your work appears.

Although publicity and marketing agencies invariably have their own cuttings services, it is a matter of courtesy to send your contacts copies of published articles featuring their products. It also ensures regular invitations to their publicity events.

## WORKING FROM PRESS RELEASES

Whether or not you receive many party invitations, you will certainly be inundated with press releases. Once on a mailing list, the information will keep on coming, although you may be asked if you would like your name removed from time to time. This can, of course, be an indication that your contact is beginning to wonder what you do with the information they send you.

### Putting the press release to good use

A press release (see the example in Figure 8) is simply a handout containing information which an organisation hopes will be given press coverage. The following is just a small selection of possible sources:

- charities

- environmental agencies

- fashion retailers

- government health and food agencies

- mail order catalogues

- manufacturing companies

- national utilities – water, power, etc.

- organisations for the disabled

- publishing houses

- sports councils

- TV production companies

- youth associations.

### Extracting the information

The press release should have a contact name and telephone number for further information. There may also be a press photo or colour transparency attached, but how much or how little you use will be governed by the length of your column.

Press Release          3 September, 1997 BRIDGEND
PEN-Y-BONT AR OGWR

## Route to the Millennium Gets Under Way

Work is set to begin on Monday on the **Newmill to Brynmenyn** section of the Ogmore Valley Community Route.

This section is a long-awaited missing link, closing the gap between the Ogmore Valley and Brynmenyn. It follows the old Ogmore Vale branch railway line which used to bring coal down from the valley to the docks.

Cyclists and walkers will soon be able to travel from Nantymoel to Aberkenfig and Sarn on a safe, traffic-free path.

Further routes are now being planned continuing down to Bridgend and linking up with the National Millennium Cyclepath stretching from Swansea to Newport.

The Ogmore Valley Community Route forms part of Groundwork Bridgend's 'Making Connections' Project funded by the Millennium Commission.

The new Community Route will be an asset to Bridgend County Borough, attracting cyclists, ramblers and nature lovers up to the year 2000 and beyond.

For further information about the Bridgend Community Route network please contact

Joanna Mole at Groundwork Bridgend, on 01656 722315.

## e n d

Groundwork Bridgend
The Environment Centre,
Maesteg Road, Tondu,
Bridgend CF32 9BT

Telephone/Ffon: 01656 722315
Fax/Ffacs: 01656 72 15 57
E.Mail: Bridgend@groundwork.org.uk

Groundwork Pen-y-bont Ar Ogw·
Canolfan yr Amgylchedd,
Heol Maesteg, Tondu,
Pen-y-bont CF32 9BT

Action for the environment

Gweithredu dros
yr amgylchedd

Note to editors:
Groundwork Bridgend is an environmental charitable trust. one of a growing network of over 40 across the UK. We operate primarily in the Bridgend County Borough area.

Groundwork's role is to work with the community, local business, local and national government to improve the environmental and economic prospects of the area.

Patron/Noddwr:
Mr Murray McLaggan. JP. MA.
Lord Lieutenant of Mid Glamorgan

GWYRDDU'R FRO
A'R CWM

GREENING THE
VALLEY & VALE

Fig. 8. Example of a press release.

Depending on the content, you may extract relevant snippets to use within the body of your own article or quote directly from the information supplied. Be aware, however, that anything you receive will have been circulated to every relevant publication, so be sure to rephrase it to suit your readership.

To gain a clearer understanding of the position with regard to press releases, study the subject matter featured in the media over one week. You will discover that the same topic, usually coinciding with a specific national event, is covered to some degree in every magazine, newspaper and general interest programme on television and radio.

Press information of this type can be utilised to fill any vacant editorial space, with the added advantage that it can be dropped at a moment's notice should something better come along.

## PLANNING AHEAD

As we have seen in the previous chapters, it always pays to plan ahead. A well-organised freelance should already know the lead times of the publications to which they regularly contribute.

### Forward thinking

Knowing that magazine and newspaper editors have to plan well in advance, be prepared for some inspired forward thinking.

Figure 4 (page 37) illustrates the format of a one-year plan for a weekly column, but you should be thinking in terms of years rather than weeks or months ahead in order to ensure topicality for issues that coincide with any of the following:

● celebrations and conferences of national, international and global significance

● anniversaries of political significance

● commemorative events of the birth/death of a famous historical figure

● the arrival/departure of an adventurer, e.g. round-the-world yachtsman, explorer, climber, etc.

With major celebrations such as the Millennium, canny editors and freelances will have been preparing material for several years before details of any planned events are made known to the public at large.

In addition to giving you the opportunity to stockpile material ready for publication as and when required, forward thinking has the added bonus of giving you the impetus to keep writing, even when markets are scarce.

*Writers News* columnist Gillian Thornton offers the following piece of advice to would-be freelances:

> Try to have the next project lined up before you finish the current one, even if it's only a filler and you're not likely to start it for ages. That way, you'll always have something to work for.

## BREAKING NEW GROUND

Once in a while, an enterprising freelance will come up with a suggestion for a column they feel is conspicuous by its absence from a particular publication.

### Creating a new market

They do so, of course, with the idea of writing the column themselves and so creating a new market for their work. As mentioned in Chapter 3, occasionally the ploy works so it is worth trying, but do take care when deciding who to approach.

Mass market publications are very carefully compiled and targeted after extensive and very expensive market research. Whilst they might be prepared to consider a 'one-off' feature or even a short series, if a leading publication has never carried a regular column along the lines you are suggesting, then it is highly unlikely that it ever will.

Alternatively, the editor of a small local newspaper or regional magazine might like your idea and be prepared to give it a trial run. It can even be possible to persuade an editor of a factual specialist magazine or local newspaper to take the occasional fictional short story.

### Providing a service for the readership

For the most part, the sort of column which might be acceptable to a local or specialist publication would be one which provides a service for the readership. This may be confined to offering regularly updated factual information or it could be in the form of interviews with enthusiasts. Whatever your idea, however, it must fit the format of the publication it is aimed at and be relevant to its readership.

## CASE STUDIES

### Beryl takes up golf

Since her retirement six months ago, Beryl has begun lessons with a golf professional. Her humorous article describing her exploits is published in a national magazine aimed at mature readers. Encouraged by this success, she writes to the editor suggesting a regular column but receives a polite refusal suggesting she approach a specialist golfing publication.

## Laura retrains for the workplace

Intending to return to work after her last child leaves home, Laura investigates the training opportunities open to mature women, but in the end, decides to work from home as a freelance writer. Using the careers information she has gathered, she sends a proposal for a series of features on women returners to a leading women's magazine which has a regular careers column. The proposal is accepted and Laura is commissioned to write three articles for the magazine.

## CHECKLIST

1. Is your manuscript easy to read?

2. Is your article designed to fit a specific magazine slot?

3. Is your article the correct length for the slot it is aimed at?

4. Do you receive press releases relevant to your area of expertise?

5. Is it possible for you to visit trade shows and make useful PR contacts?

## ASSIGNMENT

Choose a magazine column that you particularly enjoy and working from information you have to hand, see if you can write an article to fit the same slot. The article must be written:

● to length

● to the magazine's house style

● in the right format

● with an original slant.

# 11
# Marketing your Manuscript

## PRESENTING YOUR MANUSCRIPT

It is imperative that your manuscript is clean, clear and easy to read. For writers of both fact and fiction, there are a few dos and don'ts for anyone writing for publication.

### Rules for submitting manuscripts

## DO

- Establish the editorial requirements before you submit your manuscript.

- Include a brief covering letter and return postage (see Figure 9).

- Ensure that the return envelope is large enough for your manuscript.

- Type/word-process your manuscript double-spaced on one side only of A4 white paper.

- Put your name and the title of the piece at the top of each page.

- Number each page consecutively.

- Indicate that more is to follow by putting 'mf..' or 'contd./..' at the end of the page.

- Use a paperclip to keep small manuscripts together.

- Take note of any advice given in rejection letters.

- Ensure that your manuscript is neat, clean and easy to read.

- Use a dictionary to check your spelling.

- Check your manuscript through for errors before sending it off.

- Persevere – persistence does pay off.

Your name, address and telephone/fax number

Jane Smith
Editor
*Women's Magazine*
London

Dear Jane Smith

Please find enclosed a copy of a story/article entitled..............of approximately..............words which I hope you will find suitable for publication in *Women's Magazine.*

For your information, I have recently had short stories/articles published in..............and..............magazines.

Return postage is enclosed for your convenience and I look forward to hearing from you shortly.

Yours sincerely

A. N. Author

Fig. 9. Sample covering letter.

## DON'T

● Submit handwritten manuscripts.

● Forget to number each page.

● Forget to put your name and the title of the piece on each page.

● Rely on a spellchecker to correct your spelling mistakes.

● Fasten the pages together with a staple or pin.

- Put your manuscript in a plastic folder.

- Decorate your manuscript with fancy fonts and squirls.

- Use a faint typewriter or WP ribbon.

- Have your dot matrix printer permanently set on 'draft quality'.

- Leave continuous feed paper joined together with holed strips down the sides.

- Send a reply-paid return envelope too small to take your manuscript.

- Include irrelevant personal details in your covering letter.

- Send your manuscript to a totally unsuitable market.

- Telephone the editor the day after you send the manuscript to see if it arrived.

- Telephone the editor to ask why your manuscript was rejected.

- Telephone the editor *(unless they ask you to or know you personally).*

---

Your name, address and telephone/fax number




TITLE


a short story/article of approximately............words


by


name or pseudonym

---

Fig. 10. Sample front sheet for article or short story.

You can also attach a front sheet to your manuscript (see Figure 10) bearing:

● your name and address

● number of words

● preferred pen name ('by-line')

● the title.

## Choosing the right title

A title provides:

● a label for your manuscipt

● an eye-catching headline

● an idea of the content

● a hint of the tone.

It can take various forms:

● A straightforward 'How To . . .' or 'All You Need Know About . . .' heading.

● A pun, quote or misquote, e.g. 'Every Story Sells A Picture'.

● A 'shout line', e.g. 'My Husband Was A Woman!'

● A phrase from the story/article, e.g. 'For The Best'.

Due to space restrictions, it is advisable to keep titles as short as possible. For short stories, a maximum of three words is ideal.

The number of words for an article heading will vary according to the content and style, but for any titles in any genre, the three basic rules of writing apply:

● brevity

● clarity

● topicality.

Be aware, however, that whilst an imaginative title will help to catch an editor's eye, the chance that it will actually find its way into print is about 50/50.

Make sure your title clearly reflects the content of the article or story you are submitting, but don't agonise too much over it. No matter how closely you feel it reflects the magazine's style, the editor may have other ideas. Alternatively, it may be that your carefully thought-out heading simply won't fit the space available and has to be cut down to size.

## Wounding your editor

A glance through the lists of 'don'ts' above may reveal one or two points which have never occurred to you before. Not using pins or staples to fasten your manuscript, for example, because they can cause unpleasant wounds to an editor's fingers and destroy an otherwise receptive mood.

Plastic binders and folders are slippery and will cause piles of manuscripts to slide from desks whenever anyone brushes past. They also make it difficult to turn over the pages – if you are hoping to achieve publication, making life difficult for an editor is the wrong way to go about it.

All an editor really wants in a contributor is professionalism. Produce sharp, clear manuscripts on good quality white paper and regularly renew any typewriter or printer ribbons you may use.

## Printing it clearly

Dot matrix printers in particular can prove a stumbling block. The tendency of cash-conscious authors to set their printer to draft quality and re-use the fabric ribbon until it falls into holes has meant refusal by some editors to consider any manuscripts produced on dot matrix printers. If you have one, set it to 'high quality', preferably in conjunction with a non-reusable film carbon ribbon for your final copy.

One sure-fire deterrent for the discerning editor is a tightly bound manuscript, elaborately decorated with computer-generated squirls and scrolls. This smacks of a fussy amateur writing ultimately for his or her personal satisfaction, rather than a workmanlike manuscript written for the enjoyment of the reader.

## Spellchecking the manuscript

The computer program I use has an excellent spellchecker which automatically places a red wavy line under any word that I spell incorrectly. In theory, it should be foolproof, but despite the fact that there are no less than nine spelling mistakes and one punctuation error in the following passage, according to my spellchecker all the offending words are correct:

> The cliff face was shear. Donning his steal helmet, Brain prized a foothold out of the sold roc at the cliffs bass. Retching upwards, he began his assent.

A correct version is on page 138.

The errors are not, of course, in the spelling but in the context in which they are used. The hero's name, for example, could not possibly be 'Brain', it must be 'Brian', but as far as the computer is concerned, the letters are in the right order to make a recognisable word and that is all it cares about.

Unless your spellcheck program is combined with a grammar check which automatically queries contextual errors, if you are unsure about the spelling of any word, look it up in a dictionary. It may take a little longer, but the end result will be worth it and it will also confirm whether or not you are using the right word in the right place.

## Punctuating the point

One question my writing students occasionally ask is, 'Do I need to use punctuation marks when I write for publication?'

As you can see, there is a question mark at the end of that question. I put it there when I wrote it, along with all the full stops, speech marks, commas and apostrophes which adorn the pages of this book.

However, having gone through the hands of an editor whose job it is, among other things, to check grammar, not every punctuation mark has been reproduced exactly where I originally placed it.

The occasional punctuation error will not, in itself, cause an editor to reject your manuscript. However, poor punctuation and layout indicates a poor general standard of grammar and will make your work incredibly difficult to read, as the following test demonstrates:

when writing good grammar is dependent upon good punctuation as my friend Toby told me only the other day its a proven fact he declared that without speech marks commas and full stops manuscripts chances of acceptance are very small youre so right his wife Janes voice trilled its piercing tones in agreement that last one joined your other rejections so quickly it cant have been read it probably didnt even reach the editors desk I think its a crying shame.

## Laying out a manuscript

Before you attempt the above exercise, you need to bear in mind that manuscripts do not conform to standard business layouts.

Writers familiar with the blocked paragraphs and selective punctuation of today's office environment may initially find it confusing, but for anyone trained as a typist over thirty years ago, manuscript layout has hardly altered at all:

● At the beginning of each paragraph, indent approximately five spaces.

● When writing dialogue, begin a new paragraph each time a different character speaks.

All manuscripts must be typed in double-line spacing with wide margins. For feature writers, minor details like whether or not to put full stops between initial capitals will vary according to house style, but guidance should be given by your editor.

For fiction manuscripts, keep an eye on your dialogue layout and you can't go far wrong. However, do watch out for that pesky little troublemaker, the apostrophe. This is one punctuation mark which causes no end of trouble for the unwary, despite having two clearly defined functions. An apostrophe either:

● denotes a missing letter, e.g. <u>would not</u> – <u>wouldn't</u> (the apostrophe replaces the letter 'o')

or

● shows possession, e.g. <u>The girl's dress</u> – the dress belonging to the girl.

Where it causes problems is when you have a plural, for example:

● <u>The girls' dresses</u> – when the apostrophe comes after the plural 's'

or in the word 'its' when there are two alternatives:

● When 'its' is a pronoun replacing a noun, there is no apostrophe, e.g. <u>The dog's bone</u> – <u>its</u> bone.

● <u>It's</u> a lovely day – <u>it is</u> a lovely day.

Another common error is to place the apostrophe between two joined words, for example:

● <u>did not</u> should be <u>didn't</u> to denote the missing 'o' *not* <u>did'nt</u>, where the two words join.

Armed with the above information, the revised exercise should look like this:

When writing, good grammar is dependent upon good punctuation, as my friend Toby told me only the other day.

'It's a proven fact,' he declared, 'that without speech marks, commas and full stops, manuscripts' chances of acceptance are very small.'

'You're so right,' his wife Jane's voice trilled its piercing tones in agreement, 'that last one joined your other rejections so quickly, it can't have been read. It probably didn't even reach the editor's desk. I think it's a crying shame.'

## SUBMITTING YOUR WORK 'ON SPEC'

Literary agents do not, as a rule, represent short story writers, so hopeful freelances generally submit their fiction manuscripts unsolicited or 'on spec', in the hope that an editor will find them suitable for publication.

### Writing on a regular basis

Sending manuscripts to fiction editors unasked is an integral part of magazine short story writing, but there are exceptions to this. You could:

● sell your work through a syndication agency

● be asked to write a story for a specific purpose, e.g. a competition or puzzle

● be asked to write something for a new fiction slot.

Editors will contact regular contributors and work on new projects with them but as stated in an earlier chapter, probably not on a commission basis. In other words, there is no guarantee that the editor will accept the completed story.

Depending on your writing status and your professional relationship with the editor, even if the experiment is unsuccessful, you may receive a nominal fee for the work involved.

Editors are fully aware that they could be leaving you with a potentially unsaleable piece on your hands and are very sympathetic, so regard these requests as learning experiences and make the most of them. Your hard work could be rewarded with success the next time, not to mention creating a new opening for more of your stories in the future.

### Selling articles and features

In direct contrast to fiction manuscripts, it is not always advisable to send non-fiction articles and features 'on spec'.

### Sending a 'write-off'

Different editors have different requirements. Some ask new contributors to include cuttings of any previously published work, others feel this is unnecessary. Some request that you send the completed article, others prefer a brief letter outlining your idea and a 'write-off' – a short extract from your article of no more than 50 words.

Ideally you should send a stamped self-addressed envelope for contributors' guidelines or telephone to establish the editor's preference. If you do phone, keep the conversation short and never cause annoyance by insisting on speaking to the editor. A secretary or assistant can usually give you the information you require and in some cases, you need go no further than a helpful switchboard operator.

## COVERING LETTERS AND ARTICLE PROPOSALS

The sample covering letter in Figure 9 can be adapted for both short stories and factual articles.

### Keeping it short and sweet

The purpose of a covering letter is to let the editor know your name, address and telephone number, and the title and length of the piece you are submitting.

It is also a matter of common courtesy to include a polite introductory paragraph when you are contacting someone you have probably never met. You should, however, bear in mind that no matter how gentle and kind your editor's disposition, he or she will not be the slightest bit interested in your personal life. A lengthy discourse on your home, family and the reasons which led you to take up a writing career is of no consequence. All the editor wants to know is what you have submitted and whether you have any relevant experience in the publishing world.

You should certainly tell an editor if you have had any other pieces published and where they appeared. Keep it short and to the point and the editor will take you seriously.

### Setting out a proposal

Proposals for articles and series should be set out in a similar manner to the outlines for the articles themselves and include the following points:

- The subject – what the article is about.

- The content – a brief résumé.

- Background – if necessary, reference to your credentials and source material substantiating the facts.

- Details of any illustrations.

- Reader appeal – what makes you think it is suitable for the readership?

- Topicality – is it current or intended to coincide with a specific event?

The whole thing should take up no more than one sheet of paper. Ideally, you should be able to fit it all into the query letter/article proposal shown in the example in Figure 11.

Your name, address and telephone/fax number

Joe Bloggs
Editor
*Environment Magazine*
Green St
Shire

Dear Joe Bloggs

I wonder whether you would be interested in an illustrated article of approximately 1,000 words entitled Going Green.

The article offers practical advice and information on recycling not only household rubbish but also a variety of items not immediately obvious to the average homeowner.

A list of contact addresses and recycling agencies is included, together with a selection of colour slides. Publication before the end of August would coincide with the start of National Recycling Week.

I have had a number of articles published in environmental magazines and attach a copy of the most recent for your information.

Return postage is enclosed and I look forward to hearing from you shortly.

Yours sincerely

A. N. Author

Fig. 11. Sample query letter/article proposal.

## Selling the idea

Before you begin, think what the proposal is for. It is a 'selling statement' – a method of capturing an editor's interest.

Sue Preston, Senior Editor, Features of *Bella* magazine welcomes subject ideas for regular weekly features, Reports, Talking Points and

Hot Topics, but stresses that they should be accompanied by an outline of how the feature would develop.

It is up to you to convince an editor that once they agree to a feature, the article you produce will be written exactly to their specification.

## Taking advice from the professionals

Set out below are some invaluable comments from editors who have been kind enough to take the time to contribute to this book:

●   Please take the time to study a copy of *Bella* to familiarise yourself with the kind of stories we write. You'd be surprised how many would-be contributors don't! *Bella's* style of writing is quite exact, so every effort to master it is appreciated.

Sue Preston, Senior Editor, Features, *Bella*

●   Take the time to read the magazine before you send work in. There's no point sending in a short story to a magazine without a fiction section! Also, take care to spell the person's name and magazine's title correctly. Basic mistakes these!

A. Noguera, Deputy Editor, *FHM*

●   Know and understand the title you intend to write for, i.e. don't write about dogs for a cats' magazine. Thus, in the case of *The Western Mail*, articles on a general theme (as opposed to a Welsh one) are unlikely to be considered. Attempt to build up contacts at the paper/magazine/publishing house concerned and only send in unsolicited material as a last option as newsdesks/news editors/features editors have such large postbags that it can easily be lost. Write what you know readers of the publication might want to read – rather than what you want to write about – the two don't always equate with each other. Attempt to write in the style of the publication – it's all about knowing the product.

Neil Fowler, Editor, *The Western Mail*

●   It is most important that you read *Woman's Weekly* on a regular basis over several weeks before you submit your short story or serial. This is the only sure way to get the feel of our fiction.

Gaynor Davies, Fiction Editor, *Woman's Weekly*

●   Never forget who the readers are: the better the match, the easier it is to use the piece. Please do not approach us on the telephone as we simply do not have enough time to talk to people. Any approach should be in writing and be accompanied by an SAE.

Jane O'Neill, *Woman's Journal*

- If a non-fiction feature, do enclose snapshots or slides. Read several copies of the magazine and analyse type of material, length, etc.

  Jane Weatherall, *Yours*

- Read the magazine!

  Adrienne Wild, Managing Editor, *Garden Answers*

## SELECTING ALTERNATIVE MARKETS

When a short story is accepted for publication, it is important to establish exactly what rights you have sold.

The rights you should be aiming to sell are First British Serial Rights, which means that the editor is buying the right to publish your story once only in the UK in their magazine.

We'll be looking at copyright in more detail in Chapter 12, but the simple rule is that as soon as you commit an original work to paper, the copyright belongs to you. Providing you do not sell your copyright, in theory you are at liberty to resell your story again and again.

### Finding another buyer

In practice, however, it is unlikely that another UK women's magazine will want to purchase on a second, third or fourth rights basis. Therefore, if you wish to resell the piece, you will need to look at markets overseas and, of course, broadcasting opportunities.

### Resubmitting after rejection

Because the short story market is so limited, once one magazine has rejected your story, it may be difficult to place it elsewhere.

Initially, it is worth trying a similar publication, but if the same story has been rejected by any more than four UK magazines, then you need to take a long hard look at the manuscript before sending it off again.

Never be tempted to rewrite and resubmit it to an editor who has already rejected it (unless they ask you to). However, you could:

- rewrite it completely in a different style for another market

- rework the characters and rewrite the ending to suit a gentler or tougher format

- put it aside for a while so that you can return to it and rewrite it with a fresh eye

- file it away in the hope that you may eventually find a market for it

- tear it up and throw it away.

Before you resort to the last option, bear in mind that, whilst it may not be suitable for the UK market, it is possible that it may find a home overseas.

### Rewriting articles for resale

Factual articles are a far more viable proposition than short stories. Remember, there is no copyright on an idea, only the form of words in which it is expressed.

Providing you are skilled in rewriting your work to suit different styles and formats, the same basic information can be resold again and again. A topical piece could find a home in any number of different magazines, so be as flexible as you can in your writing style and one simple idea could become extremely lucrative.

However, where regional newspapers are concerned, it is best to avoid selling articles on the same topic to publications geographically close to one another, especially if their circulation areas overlap.

## OBTAINING COMMISSIONS

A commissioned piece is one that an editor has asked you to provide for a negotiated fee. Where major titles are concerned, the bulk of their material is either produced in house by staff journalists or commissioned from established authors.

For example, although *Woman's Journal* is prepared to send you editorial guidelines, Jane O'Neill points out that the majority of their material is commissioned and 'the scope for publishing unsolicited pieces is quite limited.'

An even stricter policy is operated by the *Mail on Sunday's YOU Magazine,* where editor Dee Nolan does not accept any unsolicited manuscripts but commissions all their freelance material from published professionals.

However, Jane Weatherall of *Yours* magazine is prepared to consider unsolicited fiction and factual articles which conform to the required specifications.

If you are fortunate enough to obtain a commission, make sure you have something in writing, in the form of a written offer from the editor or a letter of acceptance from you, setting out the terms agreed.

### Writing to order

It may not always be practical to write an article before it has been accepted for publication. The idea behind it may require discussion with the editor or you may be asked to provide something substantially different from your original idea.

Having accepted the terms offered, failure to produce the agreed article by the stated deadline will be a breach of contract. You must, therefore, be flexible in your approach to writing and be capable of writing to order.

Should the editor decide not to publish your article after all, you may be entitled to a 'kill fee', either the amount promised in full or a percentage payment as compensation for the work involved.

The NUJ produces a leaflet on your rights with regard to commissioned work, which can be obtained on request from: The National Union of Journalists, 314–320, Gray's Inn Road, London WC1X 8DP.

## GETTING ON-LINE

If you intend to embark on a serious career as a freelance writer, you will be expected to be computer literate. In order to be regarded as a professional and make your work instantly accessible to magazine and newspaper editors, you will need:

- a personal computer (PC)

- a modem

- a fax machine.

### Tuning into technology

When personal computers first came onto the general market, their word-processing packages were quite limited and many freelance writers took the sensible decision to purchase dedicated word processors instead.

However, technology has moved on at lightening speed and computer software is now far superior to any of those early versions. Modems, either built-in or add-on, enable you to link up with other computers via your telephone line. Fax machines are no longer considered a luxury but a necessity for the working writer and may also be a built-in feature of your computer package.

### Submitting on disk

At the present time, most magazine and newspaper editors still prefer initial submissions to be on paper, but regular contributors are invariably asked to resubmit accepted manuscripts on disk.

Editor John Lloyd of *Camping Magazine* requests that 'All written material is supplied on disk, either IBM or Mac compatible. If you work on Mac, Claris Works is the preferred word-processing program and in all other cases, Mac or IBM, the material should be presented in ASCII simple format.' In fact, it is not necessary to invest in anything too sophisticated. Most 'text editor' word-processing programs will have all the features you require. However, as I write this, far-reaching developments for the computer industry have just been announced. A cross-patent agreement between computer giant Microsoft and Apple, its much smaller but influential rival, has put an end to a long-running dispute between the two companies. Despite assurances of a commitment to the AppleMac system, news of Microsoft's $2 million plus investment in Apple is causing concern in the industry. Whilst the repercussions of any possible merger will have little impact on existing PC users, when deciding which software package to purchase in future, it might be prudent to choose one that is Microsoft compatible.

## Faxing editors

Editors will often prefer to contact regular article writers by fax rather than by phone and when a piece is required urgently, having your own fax is an economic necessity. *Bella* Features Editor, Sue Preston, prefers initial queries and sample submissions by fax to a time-consuming phone call, whilst *Yours* editor Jane Weatherall likes her contributors to have an answerphone.

E-Mail has not yet taken over, but with regional newspapers such as Wales's *Western Mail* accepting articles in this way, it cannot be too long before all topical items are submitted electronically. There is no doubt that writers reluctant to get on-line will have to fight to retain their foothold in the freelance world.

Figure 12 gives an indication of the editorial preferences from a cross-section of publications. It demonstrates at a glance the benefits to article writers of producing work on disk and having both a fax and a modem.

## SYNDICATING OVERSEAS

Once you have built up a stock of articles published FBSR in the UK, it is possible to sell them on to overseas markets.

## Selling abroad

The same market research rules apply, in that you should be familiar with the content and readership of the magazines you are aiming at.

| Title | Submitting articles on spec | | | | | Commissioned articles | | | | | |
|---|---|---|---|---|---|---|---|---|---|---|---|
| | Commission only | Unsolicited | Query letter | Whole manuscript | Manuscript (hard copy) | On disk | Fax | Modem | Payment | Rights | Illustrations |
| *You* | yes | no | no | no | | yes | yes | yes | neg. | neg. | |
| *Camping Magazine** | | yes | yes | yes | yes | yes | | | neg. | FBSR | pix/slides |
| *Bella** | | yes | or by fax | sample | yes | yes | yes | yes | varies | FBSR | Ed. arranges |
| *Woman's Journal* | usually | rarely | | yes | yes | | | | – | – | |
| *Yours* | | yes | | yes | | | yes# | | varies | FBSR | pix/slides |
| *Garden Answers** | | yes | | yes | yes | yes | yes | | neg. | All rts. | slides |
| *FHM* | | yes | +sample | | yes | yes** | yes | yes** | – | – | |
| *Western Mail* | usually | rarely | | yes | yes | yes | yes | yes | neg. | neg. | slides |

\#   Answerphone desirable
\*   Guidelines available on request + SAE
\*\*   Advisable to be on the Internet
Neg.   Negotiable

Fig. 12. Chart showing editorial policy on submission of non-fiction articles for a cross-section of magazines and newspapers.

Overseas publications are listed in the *Writers' & Artists' Yearbook* and *Willings Press Guide*, current editions of which are available in libraries (owing to recurring problems with theft, you may have to ask the librarian). You can order regular issues of the titles you select from leading suppliers or direct from the magazine's editorial office. Alternatively, if you have a friend or relative living abroad, ask them to send you a regular selection.

## Sending return postage

Return postage for overseas submissions should be in the form of International Reply Coupons (IRCs). These can be purchased from any post office and can be exchanged abroad for stamps. Make sure, however, that you send sufficient IRCs to cover the cost of returning your manuscript to you.

## Translating your work

It is not necessary to translate your manuscript into a foreign language before you submit it for publication. If an editor is willing to accept a story or article written in English, they will usually deal with translations for you, although some may require a fee for this.

## Approaching an agency

Sending your work abroad can prove very expensive in terms of postage costs, and also very time-consuming as you wait for a reply. A syndication agency is an attractive alternative, but finding the right one can be quite difficult. A list of reputable syndication agents is given in the *Writers' & Artists' Yearbook*, but this is accompanied by a warning to confirm all terms in writing before you send them your work.

There is also the problem of quantity and quality. In common with their literary agent colleagues, good syndication agents are much in demand and very selective about who they accept on their books. If you can cope with the workload yourself, it could pay dividends in terms of establishing new markets for your work on a worldwide basis.

## CHECKLIST

1.   Have you checked for punctuation and spelling mistakes?

2.   Is your manuscript clear, clean and easy to read?

3.   Have you attached return postage?

4. Can you rewrite to order?

5. Could you produce your work on disk if requested?

## ASSIGNMENT

Select a regular column in the magazine of your choice and see if you can come up with six ideas for articles which would fit the format, producing an outline for each one.

Is your manuscript clear, clean and easy to read?

# 12
# Keeping Records

## TRACKING YOUR MANUSCRIPTS

It is imperative that you keep careful track of your manuscript. Stunned by your first acceptance, you may initially feel that this is a one-off, never to be repeated fluke, bank the cheque and frame the published article for posterity.

## Becoming addicted

Be warned, however, that the thrill of seeing your work in print is addictive. Having achieved success once, the urge to try again will be irresistible and it will be essential that you know:

● which pieces have been published

● where they were published

● how much you were paid

● what copyright you sold.

## Devising a system

In the same way that you need to devise a filing system that suits you, it is necessary to come up with a user-friendly system of record-keeping.

Figure 13 is an example of a very simple method of keeping track of your manuscripts in an old-fashioned exercise book. As a back-up, a card index is still a good way to cross-reference and locate information quickly.

For some, however, the computer offers the perfect storage system and providing you make back-up copies of everything, you should be able to locate all your files at the touch of a keyboard.

| Date | Title | Publication | Format | Length | Result | Rights bought |
|------|-------|-------------|--------|--------|--------|---------------|
| 1.1.XX | For the Best | Mag A | Twist story | 1,200 wds | Accepted | F British & American SR |
| 10.1.XX | Love Charms | Mag B | Article | 1,000 wds | Accepted | FBSR |
| 23.1.XX | A Quiet Life | Mag A | Twist story | 1,200 wds | Rejected | – |
| 25.2.XX | A Quiet Life | Mag C | Twist story | 1,200 wds | Accepted | FBSR |
| 18.3.XX | Making the First Move | Mag B | Article | 850 wds | Rejected | – |
| 13.4.XX | Ten Tips for a First Date | Mag B | Article | 1,000 wds | Accepted | All Rights |
| 3.5.XX | Leaving Home | Mag D | Romance | 1,400 wds | Accepted | FBSR |

Fig. 13. Sample format for keeping track of manuscripts.

## UNDERSTANDING COPYRIGHT

Even allowing for the fact that, as soon as you write an original sentence down on paper, it becomes your copyright, it still takes an expert to understand fully this complex legal area.

### Knowing your rights

In simple terms, rights described as 'First British Serial' give the purchaser the right to publish your work in print once only in this country. By the same token:

● First French = once only in France

● First German = once only in Germany

● First American, Scandinavian and European = once only in America, Scandinavia and Europe.

### Selling your copyright

You can also sell second, third, fourth, etc. rights in the same piece, but the fee usually diminishes in proportion to the number of times the article appears in print in the same country.

You may also receive an offer to buy your manuscript on an 'All Rights For All Purposes' basis. In layman's terms, you are being asked to sell your copyright. When the piece appears in print, it will no longer be attributed to you and it can be reproduced in any format, television, radio, film, CD Rom, comic strip, etc. without any further payment or acknowledgement to you. You are, of course, under no obligation to accept this offer and can refuse, although this may result in the unceremonious return of your manuscript.

Professionals in the industry advise that you simply cross out the offending rights clause in any written offers you receive, replacing it with a note that you will only agree to the sale FBSR. Whilst this might work, it can still result in your manuscript being rejected.

## THE IMPLICATIONS OF ELECTRONIC PUBLISHING

You may wonder why major reputable publishing houses are so keen to get their hands on your copyright. There are two main reasons:

1. They can publish your work in any of their publications worldwide without making any further payment to you.

2. They can reproduce your work in electronic form worldwide without making any further payment to you.

## Assigning your copyright

Keen to exploit the possibilities in the electronic media, some of the largest magazine and newspaper publishers now have a policy of purchasing the bulk of their freelance material on an 'All Rights' basis.

This is not strictly necessary as, if they wished, they could purchase 'first rights' only in the work for both the printed and the electronic versions of their publications, thus securing the electronic rights whilst giving the freelance leeway to negotiate further payments for any subsequent rights sought.

This 'take it or leave it' attitude on the part of the publishing industry has angered increasing numbers of freelance professionals who, with the backing of the NUJ, have managed to persuade some national newspaper editors to review their purchasing policies.

## Surfing the net

Whilst the financial and legal ramifications with regard to the reproduction of material on the Internet has still to be formalised, it's not all bad news.

Dedicated net surfers are discovering a wealth of new opportunities. Requests for contributors are featured on websites and writers who can produce suitable material are E-Mailing their copy direct.

As with any other material offered for sale, it is essential to establish payment terms and duration of copyright. There is an added complication in that the Internet is worldwide, which means that it is almost impossible to put any constraint on the distribution of your material. The Authors' Licensing and Collecting Society (ALCS) suggests that one means of enabling contributors to negotiate additional payments for foreign rights is to limit the number of languages in which their material can be reproduced when it is first sold.

## Revealing the password

Electronic rights are negotiable within the terms of standard contracts and it is possible to 'password protect' your work when offering it for sale on the Internet.

Further information on writing for the electronic media is available from the Society of Authors and the ALCS. However, until an adequate monitoring system is up and running, contributors may have to be prepared to accept the risk of their payments becoming lost in cyberspace, along with their copyright.

## KEEPING ACCOUNTS – INCOME AND EXPENDITURE

Whether or not you have made any money from your writing efforts so far, you must keep a written record of every writing purchase you have made. This includes:

● stationery

● pens, pencils, sharpeners, etc.

● typewriter/printer ribbons

● ink cartridges

● sticky tape

● envelopes

● postage stamps

● paperclips

● staplers

● computer software

● reference books

● magazines for research purposes.

Anything, in fact, that you need to use in order to produce your articles and short stories.

## Buying office equipment

If you need to buy large equipment, such as a desk, chair, computer, filing cabinet, etc., this is regarded as capital expenditure for tax purposes and in common with the items listed above, can be offset against any income you receive from your writing.

Ask for a receipt for every purchase you make, including postage stamps, pencils and one-off photocopies. File them sensibly in date order and be prepared to produce them on demand if necessary.

## Banking the cheques

No matter what your financial status, you must keep a record of all the money you make from writing.

Initially, your total earnings for the financial year will probably be so small as to be insignificant, but as your success rate grows so will your income. Before long, you will find yourself hovering dangerously close to the taxable limit and unless you have allowed for the possibility of an income tax demand, you could find yourself in dire financial straits.

Payments to freelance contributors are recorded in the publisher's accounts, so keep accurate records of your income and expenditure to ensure your financial affairs are in order should your name come to the attention of the Inland Revenue.

## Invoicing magazines

Whether or not you send an invoice will depend on the purchasing policy of the magazine or newspaper concerned. In some cases, the editor simply offers a fee when they telephone to accept your manuscript and, having obtained your verbal agreement, arranges for a cheque to be issued by the accounts department. Other publications ask you to submit an invoice either to them or direct to their accounts department.

## Operating in a buyer's market

The publishing industry is a buyer's market. They dictate the terms on which they will buy your work and it is up to you to keep a sharp eye on the rights you are selling.

Some magazines may accept your manuscript on the proviso that they will pay you 'on publication'. In some instances, this can be an indication that they are in the throes of a reorganisation or that they are in financial difficulty. Either way, your piece may never actually appear in print and worse still, you may never receive the promised payment.

Payment on acceptance is far more satisfactory, but there will still be a delay whilst the authorisation goes through the magazine's accounts department. Cheques will almost certainly be issued on a set date each month, so be aware of this when you are sorting out your accounts.

## MAKING FRIENDS WITH THE TAX MAN

Now that self assessment is becoming widespread, there is plenty of advice available from the Inland Revenue on how to complete your tax form.

If you are receiving a regular income from freelance writing it may be best to register as self-employed for this purpose. Any income you receive on a PAYE basis will be recorded as before by your employer. However, it is up to you to supply the Inland Revenue with details of all your earnings, so always retain copies of invoices and payments slips on file.

## Obtaining expert advice

There may come a time when your financial affairs require the attention of an accountant. Shop around and compare quotes from a number of different firms and, if possible, try to get a recommendation from writing friends and colleagues. Accountancy fees can, incidentally, be offset against tax, so once your income reaches a sufficiently high level, an accountant could prove a worthwhile investment.

## LISTENING TO THE PROFESSIONALS

Perhaps the best way to learn about writing short stories and articles for publication is to listen to the professionals, like article and short story writer Jill Eckersley, who suggests you abide by the following three rules:

- Rule One – study the markets.

- Rule Two – Study the Markets.

- Rule Three – STUDY THE MARKETS!

She goes on to explain that, 'It doesn't matter how brilliant a writer you are, if your work isn't targeted at a particular magazine's readers, it will not sell.'

She also suggests that you 'Submit ideas for features that fit into slots in the magazine – for example, *True Life* stories or *How To* . . . features. Ask yourself who is reading this magazine? How old is she? What are her hobbies, interests, attitudes? Is she married, single, a career woman or a mum or both?'

Jill advises new authors to 'Be professional, even if this is your first attempt. A quick phone call to the editor's office will reveal whether she considers freelance contributions or prefers to see ideas/synopses, want hard copy or copy on disk. Make sure you get a proper, detailed brief and stick to it. Always keep to deadlines – if there's a problem, let the editor know in plenty of time.'

Kate Nivison, author of short stories, serials and non-fiction books urges fiction writers to 'Always read the magazine stories you are aiming for – even six stories from one magazine on a weekly basis may not be enough. Never suggest to an editor in a covering letter that "this is better" or "this one is different from your usual form" or in a similar vein, never say "X Magazine rejected this one with a nice letter, thought I'd try it with you".'

Final words of wisdom come from Gillian Thornton, who in addition to producing a regular markets column for *Writers News* magazine, writes celebrity interviews, personality pieces and general features for a wide variety of publications.

Gillian knows all too well how tough writing for publication can be. She comments that, 'Writing can be a lonely and sometimes disappointing business, even when you are well-established, so it is important to share those frustrations – and successes – with other writers. Even your nearest and dearest won't understand what it's like to have your carefully crafted prose returned with a rejection slip, but other writers can offer not only sympathy but constructive criticism too.'

Gillian advises new writers to 'Ask at your local library for details of writers' circles in the area. If there's nothing suitable, start your own. An appeal through the letters page of your local paper should soon yield some potential members. In addition, take out a subscription to *Writers News* and *Writing Magazine* to keep you in touch on a broader scale. One sale should easily pay for your subscription. Set aside a dedicated corner of your home where you can work uninterrupted, and if you are serious about selling your work, don't ever lose sight of the people you are writing for. Target every piece of work to a specific magazine and slot, so that you get into the habit of writing to style.'

She also offers encouragement in the form of this helpful tip: 'Don't forget, you don't need to be physically writing in order to be working as a writer. You can do market research by reading a magazine in bed or think of plots and ideas whilst you're doing the housework or gardening.'

My own final tip is **if you want to write, then go ahead and do it.** If you don't try, then you'll never know whether you can successfully write short stories and articles for publication.

# Solutions to Exercises

### Rewrite to reduce length
(page 25)

If you plan to bring a kitten into your home, careful preparation is vital. Your pet will need three feeding dishes, one each for water, milk and food. The water dish should have a solid base so that it won't tip up easily and must be emptied and refilled with fresh, cool water daily. (54 words)

### Answers to dialogue exercise
(page 78)

1.  Grandparent to grandchild.

2.  Hairdresser to regular client.

3.  Doctor to overworked male executive.

### Rewrite of cutting exercise
(page 100)

Alighting from the bus, she yanked the hem of her skirt to smooth out all the creases. (17 words)

### Corrected version of spelling exercise
(page 116)

The cliff face was <u>sheer</u>. Donning his <u>steel</u> helmet, <u>Brian prised</u> a foothold out of the <u>solid rock</u> at the <u>cliff's base</u>. <u>Reaching</u> upwards, he began his <u>ascent</u>.

# Glossary

**ALCS** Authors' Licensing and Collecting Society.

**Article** A factual piece written for publication in a magazine or newspaper.

**ASCII** American Standard Code for Information Interchange.

**By-line** The name you wish to appear at the end of your published article, i.e. 'written by . . .'.

**Commission** A request for a manuscript written to an agreed specification and fee.

**Conflict** Problems and emotions providing the obstacles to be overcome in short story.

**Copyright** The legal ownership of publication rights in a piece of written work.

**Dialogue** Conversation between characters.

**Double-line spacing** Leaving a blank line between each typewritten line on a page.

**Draft** First copy of a manuscript in rough, unpolished form.

**E-Mail** Electronic mail.

**Fax** Facsimile machine – enables you to send copies of manuscripts and photographs via the telephone line.

**Feature** A general interest factual article (not news).

**Fiction** A made-up story, not fact, a lie.

**Filler** A short item such as a quiz, puzzle, true fact, joke, tip, recipe, etc. which fills a space in a newspaper or magazine column.

**Flashback** A method of revealing background through snippets of information.

**Freelance** A writer who produces material on a self-employed basis for the media.

**Genre** The literary category into which your work falls.

**In-house magazine** A publication produced by a company for its employees.

**Interaction** How characters react to the people, settings and objects around them.

**IRC** International Reply Coupon.

**Letter to the editor** Letter intended for publication on a magazine or newspaper's letters page.

**Location** Where the story is set.

**Non-fiction** Fact.

**On-line** Connected to the Internet.

**On spec** Unrequested/unsolicited.

**Outline** Flexible step-by-step plan.

**PAYE** Pay As You Earn.

**Piece** A short manuscript intended for publication.

**Pix** Illustrations in the form of a photograph or colour slide/transparency.

**Press release** Publicity produced by marketing personnel for use by newspapers and magazine columnists.

**Proposal** Suggestion for a one-off article, series or serial expressed in outline format.

**Protagonist** The main character.

**Reader identification** Characters and situations which are instantly recognisable to your readership.

**Short story** A work of fiction of less than 10,000 words.

**Shout-line** Title or headline in the form of a sensational exclamation which 'shouts' or 'screams' at the reader to attract their attention.

**Showing not telling** Using interaction rather than narration to depict the sequence of events.

**Slush pile** Collection of unsolicited manuscripts waiting to be read by an editor.

**Stringer** Freelance contributor of items of news to a local newspaper.

**Syndication** To offer manuscripts for simultaneous sale to publications worldwide.

**Text editor** Computer software used as a word-processing package.

**Think piece** Non-fiction article in which the writer expresses their opinion on topical items of interest to the publication's readership.

**Unsolicited manuscript** A manuscript submitted unrequested to an editor.

**Vanity publisher** A company offering to publish your manuscript in return for payment.

# Useful Addresses

Authors' Licensing and Collecting Society, 74 New Oxford Street, London WC1A 1EF. Tel: (0171) 255 2034.

*Bella*, H. Bauer Publishing, 25–27 Camden Road, London NW1 9LL. Tel: (0171) 284 0909. Fax: (0171) 267 9835. Fiction Editor, Linda O'Byrne. Senior Editor, Features, Sue Preston.

British Library Newspaper Library, Colindale Avenue, London NW9 5HE. Tel: (0171) 636 1544.

*Camping Magazine*, Studio 9, Star Brewery, Castle Ditch Lane, Lewes, East Sussex BN7 1YJ. Tel: (01273) 477421. Fax: (01273) 477421. Editor, John Lloyd.

*FHM*, 4 Winsley Street, London W1N 7AR. Tel: (0171) 436 1515. Fax: (0171) 312 8191. Deputy Editor, A. Noguera.

*Garden Answers*, Apex House, Oundle Road, Peterborough PE2 9NP. Tel: (01733) 898100. Fax: (01733) 898433. Managing Editor, Adrienne Wild.

National Union of Journalists, Acorn House, 314–320 Gray's Inn Road, London WC1X 8DP. Tel: (0171) 278 7916.

Society of Authors, 84 Drayton Gardens, London SW10 9SB. Tel: (0171) 373 6642.

Society of Women Writers & Journalists, 110 Whitehall Road, Chingford, London E4 6DW. Tel: (0181) 529 0886.

Story Cellar, 26 Cippenham Lane, Slough, Berkshire SL1 5BS (regular short story competitions).

*The Western Mail*, Thomson House, Havelock Street, Cardiff CF1 9JN. Tel: (01222) 583583. Fax: (01222) 583652. Editor, Neil Fowler.

*Woman's Journal*, IPC Magazines Ltd., King's Reach Tower, Stamford Street, London SE1 9LS. Personal Assistant, Jane O'Neill.

*Woman's Weekly*, King's Reach Tower, Stamford Street, London SE1 9LS. Tel: (0171) 261 5000. Fax: (0171) 261 6322, Fiction Editor, Gaynor Davies.

Women Writers' Network, 55 Burlington Lane, London W4 3ET. Tel: (0181) 994 0598.

Workers Educational Association (WEA), London District, 44 Crowndale Road, London NW1 1TR. Tel: (0171) 387 8966.

Writers' Guild of Great Britain, 430 Edgware Road, London W2 1EH. Tel: (0171) 723 8074.

*Yours*, Apex House, Oundle Road, Peterborough PE2 2NP. Tel: (01733) 555123. Fax: (01733) 898847. Editorial, Jane Weatherall.

# Further Reading

*Aslib Directory of Information Sources in the UK.*
*501 Writers' Questions Answered,* Nancy Smith, Piatkus.
*Chambers Twentieth Century Dictionary.*
*Collins Electronic English Dictionary & Thesaurus.*
*Directory of Writers' Circles,* available from Oldacre, Horderns Park Road, Chapel-en-le-Frith, Derbyshire SK12 6SY.
*How to Make Money Writing Fiction,* Carole Blake, Boxtree Books.
*How to Turn Your Holidays Into Popular Fiction,* Kate Nivison, Allison & Busby.
*How to Write Horror Fiction,* William F. Nolan, Writer's Digest.
*How to Write Stories for Magazines,* Donna Baker, Allison & Busby.
*Research for Writers,* Ann Hoffman, A & C Black.
*Roget's Thesaurus,* Penguin Books.
*The Bloomsbury Guide to Grammar,* Gordon Jarvie.
*The Craft of Writing Articles,* Gordon Wells, Allison & Busby.
*The Hutchinson Concise Encyclopedia,* Century Hutchinson.
*The Magazine Writer's Handbook,* Gordon Wells, Allison & Busby.
*The Oxford Dictionary of Quotations.*
*The Writer's Digest Handbook of Short Story Writing.*
*The Writer's Handbook,* Macmillan.
*Waterhouse on Newspaper Style,* Keith Waterhouse, Penguin Books.
*Writers' & Artists' Yearbook,* A & C Black.
*Writing For Magazines,* Jill Dick, A & C Black.
*Writing For Radio,* Rosemary Horstmann, A & C Black.
*Writing Science Fiction,* Christopher Evans, A & C Black.
*Writing Step by Step,* Jean Saunders, Allison & Busby.

## How To Books in the Successful Writing series
*Copyright & Law for Writers,* Helen Shay.
*Creating a Twist in the Tale,* Adèle Ramet.
*Creative Writing,* Adèle Ramet.

*Starting to Write,* Deborah and Marina Oliver.
*Writing for Publication,* Chriss McCallum.
*Writing Romantic Fiction,* Marina Oliver.
*Writing Science Fiction, Fantasy & Horror,* Christopher Kenworthy.

**Magazines for writers**

*Freelance Market News,* Sevendale House, 7 Dale St, Manchester M29 7WL.

*Freelance Writing & Photography,* Clarendon Court, Over Wallop, Stockbridge, Hampshire SO20 8HU.

*Writers' News,* PO Box 4, Nairn IV12 4HU.

*Writing Magazine,* PO Box 4, Nairn IV12 4HU.

# Index

## CREATING A TWIST IN THE TALE

**How to write successful short stories for women's magazines**

Adèle Ramet

For the short story writer, the twist in the tale offers excellent opportunities for publication. It is fun to write and, at 500-1200 words in length, relatively economical to produce. Best of all, the market for twist stories grows with each new women's title that appears on the newsagent's shelves. However, achieving the twist in a story's tail isn't nearly so easy as it looks. Misleading by their very nature, these stories can foil attempts of even the most experienced unless they know the tricks of the trade. This book dispels the myths and misconceptions surrounding the art of writing twist stories. It will guide you step-by-step to use characterisation, viewpoint, flashback and dialogue to maximum effect. You will learn the art of 'twist signposting' and how to write backwards but most importantly of all, this book will give you all the information you need to develop that vital ingredient for success — a creatively twisted mind. Adèle Ramet is Chairman of the South Eastern Writers Association and an experienced creative writing tutor. She has contributed widely to *Bella, Woman's Realm,* and many other leading women's magazines.

*124pp. illus. 1 85703 411 2.*

## WRITING ROMANTIC FICTION

**How to make a success of your creative work**

Marina Oliver
Foreword by Joanna Trollope

Romantic fiction, in which can be included most historical novels, is the best-selling, most-borrowed type of fiction. We have all experienced love at some time, it is a universal concept, and an incredibly powerful force. It has been the theme of legends and poetry and stories throughout history. Romantic novels provide enjoyment for millions of readers. Many readers go on to write their own romantic fiction. This book helps to pinpoint the particular skills and qualities required to succeed in this very special genre. Marina Oliver, a former Chairman of the Romantic Novelists' Association, and Adviser to the latest edition of *Twentieth Century Romance and Historical Writers,* has published over thirty romances, including historicals set in different centuries and of different types, under five pseudonyms.

*128pp. illus. 1 85703 466 X.*

## COPYRIGHT & LAW FOR WRITERS

**How to protect yourself and your creative work**

Helen Shay

This book will be a useful tool for any writer, but especially invaluable to beginners and those just starting to enjoy some success. Make sure you never receive any legal short change. This book takes you through the main legal implications relevant to writers, from first putting pen to paper/finger to keyboard through to selling work, entering a contract and onto collecting the full financial rewards due to you. It also explains exactly what to do if things go wrong. It explains the various pitfalls and how to steer clear of them — for example copyright infringement — whilst showing how to preserve your own rights, and learning how to publish and not be damned. A graduate of Manchester University, Helen Shay is a qualified solicitor of twelve years' standing. Currently working in an ombudsman's office in London, she is well-versed in the problems which can confront the individual versus large organisations. She also tutors and lectures part-time in business law. She is a member of the Society of Women Writers and Journalists and the Women Writers Network, and currently writes a regular legal column for *Writers News*.

*96pp. illus. 1 85703 416 3.*


## WRITING & SELLING A NOVEL

**How to craft your fiction for publication**

Marina Oliver

Writing a novel seems a daunting task until attempted. Marina Oliver's invaluable, eminently practical book, based on firsthand experience, offers realistic encouragement, down to earth advice, expert tips and suggestions to guide aspiring novelists. They include how to get started, the key elements to consider, where to look for help, how to approach publishers and what to expect during the process of publication. A former further education lecturer, and tutor for creative writing courses, Marina Oliver has published over 30 novels, short, long, historical and contemporary. Chairman of the Romantic Novelists' Association 1991-3, and an adviser to the 1994 edition of the biographical dictionary, *Twentieth Century Romance and Historical Writers*, she lectures widely on writing.

*144pp. illus. 1 85703 406 6.*

## WRITING REVIEWS

**How to write about arts and leisure for pleasure and profit**

Carole Baldock

Imagine enjoying all your favourite leisure activities for free — eating out and visiting tourist attractions, going to exhibitions and concerts, theatre and cinema, or being entertained in the comfort of your own home with new books, CDs and the latest video releases. Newspapers and magazines of all kinds have a huge appetite for reviews, much of which is written by freelancers. This book shows you how to break into the reviewing market, how to set up, how to conduct research and interviews, how to draft your review and tailor it to the appropriate media, and how to use reviewing for personal networking and skills-building. Carole Baldock BA(Hons) is herself a highly experienced freelance reviewer whose work has appeared throughout the national and provincial press and in specialist publications of many kinds.

*160pp. illus. 1 85703 441 4.*

## HOW TO WRITE FOR TELEVISION

**A complete guide to writing and marketing TV scripts**

William Smethurst

Television is a huge and expanding market for the freelance writer. Particularly in the field of drama, producers are constantly looking for new writers for situation comedies, series drama, and soap operas and single plays. But what kind of scripts are required? How should a script be presented and laid out? What camera moves should you put in, and should you plan for commercial breaks? Which programmes and organisations should you contact, and which are the subjects to tackle or avoid? Packed with hard-hitting information and advice, and illustrated throughout with examples, this is a complete step-by-step manual for every writer wanting to break into this lucrative market. 'Packed with information which is well presented and easily accessible.' *National Association of Careers & Guidance Teachers Bulletin.* 'If would-be TV scriptwriters are looking for a wide ranging and practical book to light the fuse which could lead to a successful career, they should certainly invest in a copy of William Smethurst's *How to Write for Television.*' *BAFTA News.* 'Your best starting point is probably William Smethurst's book.' *Writers News.* William Smethurst has been a television script editor at BBC Pebble Mill, and executive producer of drama serials for Central Television. He is now a director of the independent television company, Andromeda Television Ltd.

*160pp illus. 1 85703 045 1.*

## STARTING TO WRITE

### How to create written work for publication and profit

Marina & Deborah Oliver

How does a writer get started? How do writers manage the physical aspects? This book shows would-be writers how to look at their motives, how to set realistic objectives, and how to devise a plan of action without wasting time and resources. Illustrated throughout with case studies, it will show you how to explore various options, discover what methods work best for you, and take advantage of tips from experienced writers. Start now, and learn how to get your work into print. Marina Oliver has written and published over 30 novels, published her own magazine, written and edited many booklets, and taught creative writing. Deborah Oliver has edited a monthly magazine and is currently production editor of a computer magazine.

*124pp. illus. 1 85703 401 5.*


## WRITING FOR PUBLICATION

### Your practical guide to success

Chriss McCallum

'How can I sell my work? How do I protect my copyright? Can a magazine steal my story? Why just a printed rejection slip — can't editors tell me where I'm going wrong? Are writing courses worth the money? Should I get an agent?' Highly expert and practical, *Writing for Publication* gives the often surprising answers to these and hundreds of other questions most often asked by the great silent majority of struggling writers, whether of fiction, nonfiction, poetry, drama, stories or articles. No author seriously interested in getting published can afford to be without this manual, packed with checklists, examples and key contacts. 'Handy for both professional and newcomer alike.' *Writers News.* 'Everything you ever wanted to know about the practical side of publishing . . . excellent.' *Competitors Journal.* 'Really definitive . . . Leaves every other similar book in its shade.' *Pause (National Poetry Foundation).* 'It is, quite simply, one of the best books of its kind that I've ever read.' Steve Wetton, author of BBC TV's comedy drama *Growing Pains.* 'The revised edition maintains the high standard . . . Its reference section of useful addresses is value for money on its own.' *Writers News.* Chriss McCallum has many years' experience as a professional editor, and has worked for Collins, Penguin, W H Allen and other leading firms. She was publisher of *The Writers Voice* (1983-86) and is a Member of the Society of Authors, The Society of Women Writers & Journalists, and an Honorary Member of the Comedy Writers Association.

*192pp illus. 1 85703 226 8. 4th edition.*

# How To Books

How To Books provide practical help on a large range of topics. They are available through all good bookshops or can be ordered direct from the distributors. Just tick the titles you want and complete the form on the following page.

___ Apply to an Industrial Tribunal (£7.99)
___ Applying for a Job (£8.99)
___ Applying for a United States Visa (£15.99)
___ Backpacking Round Europe (£8.99)
___ Be a Freelance Journalist (£8.99)
___ Be a Freelance Secretary (£8.99)
___ Become a Freelance Sales Agent (£9.99)
___ Becoming a Father (£8.99)
___ Buy & Run a Shop (£8.99)
___ Buy & Run a Small Hotel (£8.99)
___ Buying a Personal Computer (£9.99)
___ Career Networking (£8.99)
___ Career Planning for Women (£8.99)
___ Cash from your Computer (£9.99)
___ Choosing a Nursing Home (£9.99)
___ Choosing a Package Holiday (£8.99)
___ Claim State Benefits (£9.99)
___ Collecting a Debt (£9.99)
___ Communicate at Work (£7.99)
___ Conduct Staff Appraisals (£7.99)
___ Conducting Effective Interviews (£8.99)
___ Coping with Self Assessment (£9.99)
___ Copyright & Law for Writers (£8.99)
___ Counsel People at Work (£7.99)
___ Creating a Twist in the Tale (£8.99)
___ Creative Writing (£9.99)
___ Critical Thinking for Students (£8.99)
___ Dealing with a Death in the Family (£9.99)
___ Do Your Own Advertising (£8.99)
___ Do Your Own PR (£8.99)
___ Doing Business Abroad (£10.99)
___ Doing Business on the Internet (£12.99)
___ Doing Voluntary Work Abroad (£9.99)
___ Emigrate (£9.99)
___ Employ & Manage Staff (£8.99)
___ Find Temporary Work Abroad (£8.99)
___ Finding a Job in Canada (£9.99)
___ Finding a Job in Computers (£8.99)
___ Finding a Job in New Zealand (£9.99)
___ Finding a Job with a Future (£8.99)
___ Finding Work Overseas (£9.99)
___ Freelance DJ-ing (£8.99)
___ Freelance Teaching & Tutoring (£9.99)
___ Get a Job Abroad (£10.99)
___ Get a Job in Europe (£9.99)
___ Get a Job in France (£9.99)
___ Get a Job in Travel & Tourism (£8.99)
___ Get into Radio (£8.99)
___ Getting a Job in America (£10.99)
___ Getting a Job in Australia (£9.99)
___ Getting into Films & Television (£10.99)
___ Getting That Job (£8.99)
___ Getting your First Job (£8.99)
___ Going to University (£8.99)
___ Having a Baby (£8.99)

___ Helping your Child to Read (£8.99)
___ How to Study & Learn (£8.99)
___ Investing in People (£9.99)
___ Investing in Stocks & Shares (£9.99)
___ Keep Business Accounts (£7.99)
___ Know Your Rights at Work (£8.99)
___ Learning to Counsel (£9.99)
___ Live & Work in Germany (£9.99)
___ Live & Work in Greece (£9.99)
___ Live & Work in Italy (£8.99)
___ Live & Work in Portugal (£9.99)
___ Live & Work in the Gulf (£9.99)
___ Living & Working in America (£12.99)
___ Living & Working in Australia (£12.99)
___ Living & Working in Britain (£8.99)
___ Living & Working in China (£9.99)
___ Living & Working in Hong Kong (£10.99)
___ Living & Working in Israel (£10.99)
___ Living & Work in New Zealand (£9.99)
___ Living & Working in Saudi Arabia (£12.99)
___ Living & Working in the Netherlands (£9.99)
___ Living Away From Home (£8.99)
___ Making a Complaint (£8.99)
___ Making a Video (£9.99)
___ Making a Wedding Speech (£8.99)
___ Manage a Sales Team (£8.99)
___ Manage an Office (£8.99)
___ Manage Computers at Work (£8.99)
___ Manage People at Work (£8.99)
___ Manage Your Career (£8.99)
___ Managing Budgets & Cash Flows (£9.99)
___ Managing Credit (£8.99)
___ Managing Meetings (£8.99)
___ Managing Projects (£8.99)
___ Managing Your Personal Finances (£8.99)
___ Managing Yourself (£8.99)
___ Market Yourself (£8.99)
___ Mastering Book-Keeping (£8.99)
___ Mastering Business English (£8.99)
___ Master GCSE Accounts (£8.99)
___ Master Public Speaking (£8.99)
___ Migrating to Canada (£12.99)
___ Obtaining Visas & Work Permits (£9.99)
___ Organising Effective Training (£9.99)
___ Passing Exams Without Anxiety (£8.99)
___ Passing That Interview (£8.99)
___ Plan a Wedding (£8.99)
___ Planning Your Gap Year (£8.99)
___ Preparing a Business Plan (£8.99)
___ Publish a Book (£9.99)
___ Publish a Newsletter (£9.99)
___ Raise Funds & Sponsorship (£7.99)
___ Rent & Buy Property in France (£9.99)
___ Rent & Buy Property in Italy (£9.99)
___ Research Methods (£8.99)

# How To Books

___ Retire Abroad (£8.99)
___ Return to Work (£7.99)
___ Run a Voluntary Group (£8.99)
___ Setting up Home in Florida (£9.99)
___ Setting Up Your Own Limited Company (£9.99)
___ Spending a Year Abroad (£8.99)
___ Start a Business from Home (£7.99)
___ Start a New Career (£6.99)
___ Starting to Manage (£8.99)
___ Starting to Write (£8.99)
___ Start Word Processing (£8.99)
___ Start Your Own Business (£8.99)
___ Study Abroad (£8.99)
___ Study & Live in Britain (£7.99)
___ Studying at University (£8.99)
___ Studying for a Degree (£8.99)
___ Successful Grandparenting (£8.99)
___ Successful Mail Order Marketing (£9.99)
___ Successful Single Parenting (£8.99)
___ Survive Divorce (£8.99)
___ Surviving Redundancy (£8.99)
___ Taking in Students (£8.99)
___ Taking on Staff (£8.99)
___ Taking Your A-Levels (£8.99)
___ Teach Abroad (£8.99)
___ Teach Adults (£8.99)
___ Teaching Someone to Drive (£8.99)
___ Travel Round the World (£8.99)
___ Understand Finance at Work (£8.99)
___ Use a Library (£7.99)
___ Using the Internet (£9.99)

___ Winning Consumer Competitions (£8.99)
___ Winning Presentations (£8.99)
___ Work from Home (£8.99)
___ Work in an Office (£7.99)
___ Work in Retail (£8.99)
___ Work with Dogs (£8.99)
___ Working Abroad (£14.99)
___ Working as a Holiday Rep (£9.99)
___ Working as an Au Pair (£8.99)
___ Working in Japan (£10.99)
___ Working in Photography (£8.99)
___ Working in the Gulf (£10.99)
___ Working in Hotels & Catering (£9.99)
___ Working on Contract Worldwide (£9.99)
___ Working on Cruise Ships (£9.99)
___ Write a Press Release (£9.99)
___ Write & Sell Computer Software (£9.99)
___ Write for Television (£8.99)
___ Writing a CV that Works (£8.99)
___ Writing a Non Fiction Book (£9.99)
___ Writing a Report (£8.99)
___ Writing a Textbook (£12.99)
___ Writing an Assignment (£8.99)
___ Writing an Essay (£8.99)
___ Writing & Publishing Poetry (£9.99)
___ Writing & Selling a Novel (£8.99)
___ Writing Business Letters (£8.99)
___ Writing for Publication (£8.99)
___ Writing Reviews (£9.99)
___ Writing Romantic Fiction (£9.99)
___ Writing Science Fiction (£9.99)
___ Writing Your Dissertation (£8.99)

---

To: Plymbridge Distributors Ltd, Plymbridge House, Estover Road, Plymouth PL6 7PZ.
Customer Services Tel: (01752) 202301. Fax: (01752) 202331.

Please send me copies of the titles I have indicated. Please add postage & packing (UK £1, Europe including Eire, £2, World £3 airmail).

☐ I enclose cheque/PO payable to Plymbridge Distributors Ltd for £ [        ]

☐ Please charge to my ☐ MasterCard, ☐ Visa, ☐AMEX card.

Account No. [                              ]

Card Expiry Date [    ] 19  ☎ Credit Card orders may be faxed or phoned.

Customer Name (CAPITALS) ........................................................

Address ...........................................................................

........................................................ Postcode ...............

Telephone ........................... Signature ...........................

Every effort will be made to despatch your copy as soon as possible but to avoid possible disappointment please allow up to 21 days for despatch time (42 days if overseas). Prices and availability are subject to change without notice.

Code BPA